REMEMBERING THE WORLD WAR II SACRIFICE:

DAD'S LETTERS

Remember their sacrifice

By Joel E. Houglum

ISBN: 978-1-57579-424-2

Library of Congress Control Number: 2010905362

Copies of this book are available at:
http://WWIIDadsLetters.com

Printed in the United States of America

PINE HILL PRESS
4000 West 57th Street
Sioux Falls, SD 57106

To the grandchildren who knew Dad, and to the generations
of great grandchildren who never will,
that they all will appreciate the price of freedom.

Dad and Mom with their grandchildren, 1986.

Ten of Dad and Mom's twelve great-grandchildren, 2009.

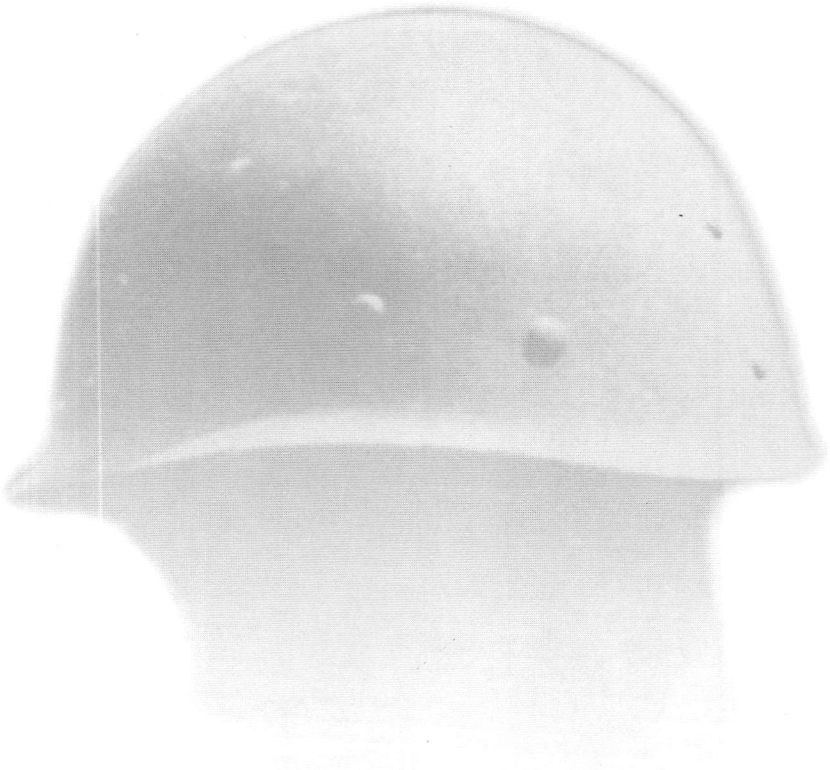

Table Of Contents

Acknowledgements

I am very grateful to several people for assisting me in this endeavor and want to express my heartfelt "thank you" to:

My Uncle Jim and Aunt Harriet, and Aunt Thelma for filling in some details that only they would know, identifying people in old pictures, and sharing their past.

Harry Libby for providing much information regarding the 324th Regiment, offering suggestions for other sources of information, being the secretary for the Wildcat News, and for being such an enthusiastic advocate for the men of the 324th Regiment ("Let's Go").

John Kregel for providing quotes from his interview with Dad in 2000.

Kathy Spolum for reviewing the manuscript for spelling, grammar, and punctuation.

My wife, Rita, for her encouragement and many helpful comments regarding the manuscript.

All the relatives, friends, and neighbors who wrote Dad while he was in the Army, sent him packages and cards, or prayed for his safe return. They all had an impact on Dad's life, and now mine, to an extent that they could not imagine.

Dad's children and grandchildren, thanking them in advance, for keeping the memory of Dad and the World War II sacrifice alive in the hearts of their children and grandchildren.

Author's Notes

Story of One

This is the story of one man, his sacrifice for his country, how World War II changed the course of his life, and how his life left a lasting imprint on his family, community, and country. Even though the book focuses on my dad, it is similar to the stories of many other soldiers who have served this great country. Some soldiers suffered more; some less, but they all sacrificed.

Transcription of Letters

This book contains the transcription of many personal letters written in the 1940s. To maintain the authenticity of these letters, spelling or grammar errors have not been corrected nor noted within the transcription unless there was some uncertainty regarding the writer's spelling or intent, or if the reader most likely would think an error in transcription had occurred. In some cases, clarification of terminology or identity of a person being referred to in the letter is added in brackets [ ]. Maintaining spelling or grammar errors, slang terms, or personal information within the transcription is not intended to be a negative reflection on the letter writers, who never expected that the content of their letters would be used in this manner. The purpose is to give an accurate account of what the writers intended and to give credit to these people who gave of themselves through letters as a means of comforting and encouraging Dad during the time that he was serving his country. I hope in some way, seeing the importance of these letters to Dad will inspire family and friends to maintain frequent contact with men and women currently in the military who are away from home.

Distances Between Cities

Some chapters contain estimation of miles between certain points that Dad traveled during World War II. Generally, these were measured as air miles from point A to point B by using maps available on various Internet sites. The intent is to give the reader a general idea of the distances involved and are not intended to represent actual distances traveled by land that would invariably include winding roads or mountainous terrain.

Preface

Edgar J. Houglum, February 6, 1922 – August 6, 2006; that was Dad's life time. He lived his entire adult life in Twin Valley, Minnesota; population about 1,000. During World War II he earned the Silver Star, Bronze Star, Purple Heart and Cluster, Good Conduct Medal, European Theatre of Operations Medal, American Defense Medal, and Victory Medal. He was honorably discharged from the Army in 1947 as a first lieutenant. He was faithful to his family and to his wife of over fifty years, and he served his community for over fifty years in many capacities. Until the renewed public interest in World War II occurred near the 50-year anniversary of D-Day and VE-Day, Dad's heroic service to his country was not publicized, and like so many veterans, he did not talk about it. I'm sure he felt like many of his comrades who returned from the war that the 425 men from his regiment who never made it back to the United States were the heroes.

February 6, 1922 – August 6, 2006

After the war, many veterans settled in small towns and worked to build and maintain the vitality of those small towns through their commitment to the community and to their families. These are the quiet, small-town heroes.

These men didn't tout the heroism of their own service. They gave brave service to their country and continued with faithful service to their families and communities. Those of us who are not veterans will never know what these men suffered throughout the war, what they endured from those memories for years, and the extent to which the events of World War II changed their lives.

One Veteran's Day, I told Dad that I would do my best to ensure that his sacrifice for his country would not be forgotten by his grandchildren and great grandchildren. This book is meant to help keep that promise. With the aid of letters that Dad wrote and received while serving in the Army, this book chronicles much of Dad's military life and reveals some of his character traits that were innate in so many brave soldiers. These traits contributed to the victory in World War II. The sacrifices of these men changed the course of their lives beyond measure, including the life of my dad, Edgar J. Houglum.

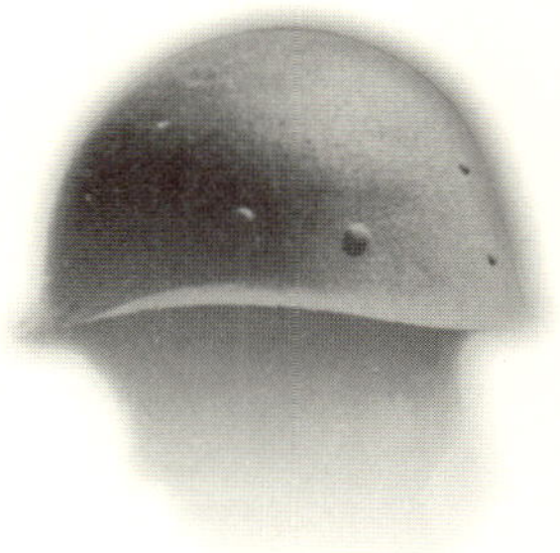

Chapter One

How Dad Turned Out

My four sisters and one brother, our spouses, children and grandchildren sat in the front pews in St. William's Catholic Church in Twin Valley, Minnesota. This was the church my siblings and I had attended while growing up. Although we were more accustomed to the old, white church building next door, which was no longer used for church services, this new brick church, with a modern interior and larger sanctuary, was fairly familiar to us since we had been in it many times when we visited our parents. It was August 12, 2006, Dad's funeral service.

My dad, Edgar Jesness Houglum, had passed away in his sleep on August 6th. For me it was one of those occasions that you will always remember where you were when you heard the news: a Kennedy assassination-like event, only much more personal. We had just seen Dad the week before at my nephew's wedding in Wisconsin. In fact, most of his children, grandchildren, and great grandchildren were at Benj and Hannah's wedding, as were many other relatives. The week following the wedding, Dad and my oldest sister, Peggy, traveled to Michigan and Wisconsin visiting my other sisters (Pam, Joan, and Deanna) and a few other relatives before returning to Twin Valley. Dad seemed to be in relatively good health and spirits, so his death came as a shock to us all.

We were blessed to see so many community residents, former classmates of ours, friends, and family in attendance at the funeral, some of whom traveled many miles from Minnesota and North Dakota to be there; one cousin flew from Colorado to pay his respects.

The funeral service was planned by the family. Our cousins Gregg, Tom, and Bruce, took part in the music just as they had seven years earlier for our mother's funeral, which made the service even more emotional for us. In fact, we planned much of the ceremony to be the same as my mother's: the church organist, Monica, was a favorite of my parents, the pallbearers were the same grandchildren, the interment was at the same cemetery. However, a different priest, Father Friedl, officiated over the service, including the homily. He was relatively new to the church in Twin Valley and thus unfamiliar to me and my siblings. I remember wondering how well he would be able to relate to Dad's life and his family, having only known Dad for a short time, but I was very pleased with what he had to say.

It is funny what things go through your mind during emotionally stressful times. The statement in Father Friedl's homily that stuck in my head was that Dad was born in 1922, and "now we see how his life turned out." Typically at funerals the only mention of how the deceased "turned out" is the short description in the funeral program. Dad's obituary in the program gave some information about his military service, and his commitment to his community, church, and family. Beyond that short description, how did Dad's life "turn out"?

Commitment

If anyone was about being committed, it was Dad. He had lived in the same house fifty-seven years, building most of the interior himself. Dad was married to Mom for over fifty-one years. When Mom developed Alzheimer's disease, Dad never mentioned how bad the disease had progressed, but continued to take care of her at home. Only at my urging and those of my siblings, did Dad finally place Mom in a nursing home; that's where they celebrated their 50th wedding anniversary. Yes, Dad was committed; he visited Mom daily until her death on Valentine's Day, 1999.

Dad's commitment extended to his community and church which he served in many ways:

- He was a member of the Lion's Club for over 45 years.
- He served as the Twin Valley Lions secretary-treasurer for 36 years.
- He sponsored over 30 new members to the Lion's Club.
- He served on 13 Lion's Club district cabinets.

- He was the secretary-treasurer of the Twin Valley Bowling Association for 25 years.
- He was the treasurer of the Twin Valley One Fund Drive for 7 years.
- He was a church council member for 12 years.
- He served in various capacities in several other organizations, including the American Legion, the VFW, the Disabled American Veterans, the National Rural Mail Carriers Association, the Retired Officers Association, and the Knights of Columbus.
- He worked part time as City Clerk for 8 years.

Doing his best was part of Dad's character; it's a component of being committed. That was notable during his military career but also evident in his job as a rural mail carrier that he held for thirty-six years. Although the length of his mail route increased as years passed, it started as 54.9 miles. I remember on many occasions during the winter, to the delight of us kids, school was cancelled for the day due to the blowing and drifting snow. Regardless of the weather, however, Dad would have the car loaded with the mail and would do his best to get it distributed to all the rural patrons on his route. Oftentimes he would have chains on the back wheels of his 1930 Model A Ford, the car he bought when he started hauling mail, and have me accompany him to help him if he got stuck in snow drifts. Visibility would be bad, snow would be drifted across the road in many places, and we would get stuck a few times before getting back to town. It wasn't often that he had to give up and turn around.

The 1930 Model A Ford used by Dad during his days as a rural mail carrier. Picture taken on Dad's last day delivering mail by Leonard Bakke, a long-time patron on Dad's route.

The farm families to whom Dad delivered mail were grateful for his efforts, and sometimes they would help him out by plowing snow from a stretch of road before his arrival. For some families, he delivered mail to five generations. He certainly was the epitome of what has often been quoted as the U.S. Postal Service slogan, *"Neither snow nor rain nor heat nor gloom of night stays these couriers from the swift completion of their appointed rounds."* When Dad retired he received recognition for driving over a million miles without a single accident.

Dad's commitment to the community and to his church was well known by his family and most of the other long-time residents of Twin Valley. This is how his life "turned out," and we all knew it. During the few days preceding the funeral when we began the process of making funeral arrangements, getting his financial affairs in order, and buying various items in the shops around town, the respect that the community had for Dad quickly became evident. The people in our home town brought food to the house, stopped by to tell us their stories of why Dad was important to them, aided us in making funeral arrangements, and offered their homes for us to stay as the number of our immediate family members gathering in Twin Valley was increasing. Repeatedly we heard how Dad was a quiet and gentle person who was highly respected by everyone because he had been committed to his family, community, and country. They all knew how his life had turned out. Oddly, I had never thought of him as a quiet and gentle man; I had just thought of him as "Dad."

My siblings and I knew much of the detail of Dad's community involvement; after all, he was living that part of his life when we lived at home. But we did not know much about his military life. We knew that he had several medals because we each had seen them on several occasions. They were kept in a grey combination safe that was about one cubic foot. The safe was so heavy that it never moved from its appointed spot on the floor of our parent's bedroom closet (Dad's side). When we were youngsters, whenever Dad would open the safe, one or more of us kids would be there to take out his army medals, open their individual cases and look at them. He never displayed them until the last few years of his life. Dad rarely talked about specific experiences of the war, and we never saw any of the letters written during his military career until after his death. We did not know much of the specifics of how his life "turned out" during the war. Several years prior to his death, I gave him a tape recorder and asked him to record any specific events of the war that came to his mind; he never recorded a word. I did not know what questions to ask, and not wanting to force unwanted thoughts to the surface, I did not probe.

Patriotism

Being patriotic was an expectation in our house; it was one of those no-brainer ideals that were taught by parents and schools along with respect for elders, being polite to others, respecting the flag, and being honest. The Pledge of Allegiance was a daily routine to begin each class day in grade school. Dad's patriotism was evident by his military service and continued involvement in the VFW and American Legion.

In our small town, each Memorial Day included a short parade, which ended at the town cemetery with a ceremony of remembrance for all deceased community members who had served our country. Among the parade participants were color guard and rifle corps comprised of VFW and American Legion members who marched in their military uniforms to the cemetery.

After the Memorial Day ceremony, it was often the case that our family would have a picnic, usually in the back yard. But Dad missed our Memorial Day lunch virtually every year because he went with other VFW and American Legion members to the countryside cemeteries in the area to perform a similar service. Not that he was fond of picnics anyway since, as he put it, he had enough eating outside during the war (he also said the same thing about camping). Picnics aside, he continued to perform this patriotic duty for many, many years. Like the other local veterans, he was dedicated to honoring the deceased comrades.

Granddaughter, Catherine, with her grandfathers who served in the Army. Each grandfather pinned one of Dad's Second Lieutenant's gold bars on Cate's uniform at this pinning and commissioning ceremony, May 2001.

Another patriotic act that was most unique to Dad occurred in May 2001. Our daughter, Cate, graduated from South

Dakota State University and was commissioned into the Army as a second lieutenant. Dad had offered his lieutenant's gold bars to Cate for her to wear on her uniform. So she asked Dad and her Grandpa Scully, who also had served in the Army during World War II, to pin the bars on her during the pinning ceremony. What a proud day for the family, seeing Cate's two grandfathers, one at each of her shoulders, pinning my Dad's gold bars onto her uniform. During the four years that Cate was in the Army, her military service was an additional point of connection for the two of them. It was a unique bond between grandfather and granddaughter.

Last Salute

Now it was five years later and Cate had one more military service she needed to perform for Dad, a last connection between her and Dad. When the funeral service was over, we drove to the town cemetery. It only took a few minutes to drive the five blocks. My Dad was to be buried next to Mom and near the twin boys, Michael Carl and Mitchell Craig, who had died hours after birth in May 1958. The canopy and family seating area was all set up. It was a nice August day. After the short ceremony by the priest, an emotional few minutes followed. The son of my youngest sister, Deanna, had served in the Navy, so he and Cate had agreed to take care of the flag. Both served during the beginning of the second war with Iraq. They had agreed that since Cate had presented the flag to her grandmother when Cate's Grandpa Scully passed away, Tony would present the flag to the oldest of Dad's children, Peggy.

Dad was proud of the military service of these two grandchildren, and he would have been proud of how well they performed their duty that day. They looked sharp in their uniforms, Tony in his Navy Dress Blue and Cate in Army Dress Green. The 21-rifle salute rang out to honor a fallen comrade, followed by "Taps." Cate and Tony then removed the American Flag that was draped over Dad's casket and folded it without a misstep, and Tony was able to ceremoniously recite the verse without emotionally breaking, *"On behalf of the President of the United States and the people of a grateful nation, may I present this flag as a token of appreciation for the honorable and faithful service your loved one rendered this nation."* He said later that he knew he could not look directly at Aunt Peg and keep his composure. The lump in my throat exists today whenever I relive these emotional events. Dad was dead, but patriotism was alive and living in the hearts of his family!

Remembering

After Dad's funeral and gravesite ceremony, and after the lunch reception at the church, a few relatives joined us at Dad's house for some more conversation. Eventually the day of remembering Dad ended. Throughout an exhausting day, people had gone out of their way to do seemingly little things that became a significant part of the whole event, including a cousin who retrieved a rifle shell from the rifle salute and gave it to me as a keepsake of Dad's last military connection; a friend who gathered the roses from the coffin and delivered them to the house along with the instructions on how to have them made into bracelets and necklaces as keepsakes; and the church ladies who served us food with words of encouragement. People doing things for our family made the day easier.

Remembrances of both Mom and Dad continued as we took care of the affairs of the house. It is an odd experience to filter through a parent's personal effects: wallet, chest of drawers, valuable papers, insurance policies, and bank accounts. Doing so we found many letters written to Dad from friends and relatives during his military service, and letters that he wrote to his parents during that same time period. As I read these letters, it was like hearing Dad speaking again. Some letters gave insight as to what he was thinking and feeling while serving his country, whereas others revealed the character that he exemplified throughout his life.

As I used Dad's letters to follow the path of his military career, I gained a greater appreciation of the sacrifice he paid for his country so that we could have the freedoms we enjoy today. It also helped me realize the impact those four years had on his remaining sixty years. No doubt all wars have an impact on the futures of all who sacrificed. If so, then Dad's story is the story of many.

I won't forget Dad, but it is important to me that his grandchildren not forget him, and that the many great grandchildren who never knew him not “forget” him either. If they feel connected to one who sacrificed, maybe they will appreciate the many who sacrificed for their country. If Dad’s great grandchildren know him better through this book, maybe the way Dad “turned out” will be his legacy to them: a model of patriotism and good character.

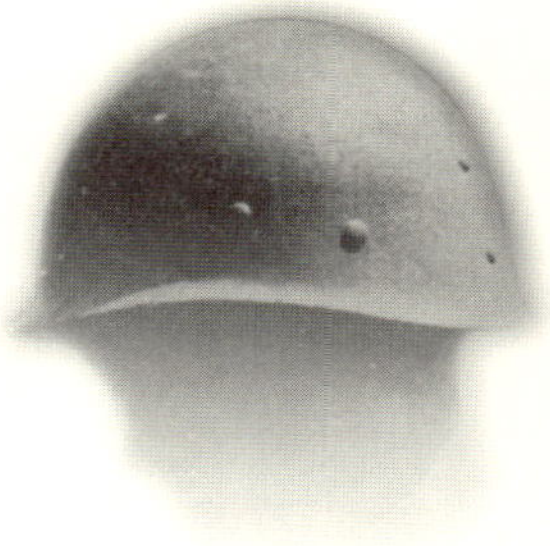

Chapter Two

Early Foundation

Dad was born February 6, 1922, in Waubun, Minnesota, to (Carl) Edward and Alma Houglum. He was the middle child of three sons; (Victor) Monroe, born June 26, 1920, and James, born April 4, 1924.

The Farm

The Houglum family farm house was built in 1911. It is located about seven miles west of Waubun and three miles northeast of Flom. My great grandfather, Lars, was the original owner and although he helped build it, according to Dad it was my great grandfather's son-in-law, Joe Bement, who did most of the construction.

My grandparents, Edward and Alma, lived on the Houglum family farm when they were first married. My grandmother was a school teacher before she was married, and she taught at the Cheerful Nook country school located about a mile north of the Houglum farm. She stayed at the farmhouse while teaching at Cheerful Nook and that is how she met my grandfather. (Coincidently, that is how Monroe met his wife, Thelma, many years later as she stayed at the Houglum farm while teaching at Cheerful Nook.)

After Monroe was born, my grandparents moved to Waubun where Dad was born. My grandmother had family (Jesness) living in Fosston, Minnesota, so in an effort to find work for my grandfather, the family moved to Fosston where the third son, Jim, was born. In the fall of 1930, again in an effort for my grandfather to find a job, the family moved to International Falls where my grandfather had family. He managed a grocery store for a short time, but the grocery business didn't work out

Houglum farm house built in 1911. Dad's paternal grandparents (left), Lars and Kari, with some of their children and grandchildren, 1912. Children and grandchildren, left to right: Leo, between grandparnts, Leona and Emma Bement, Clara Houglum, Mary Bement, and Alice Houglum.

as anticipated, so the family moved back to Fosston in time for the boys to complete the second half of the school year there. In the fall of 1931, when Dad was nine years old, the family made a final move back to the family farm as it became part of the family inheritance.

The farm house was a two-story building with a narrow and steep stairway leading upstairs to four rooms. When my siblings and I were kids, the smaller northwest bedroom was used for storage. On several occasions we rummaged around for treasures. We came across military memorabilia (e.g., army hat, dried up K-rations, German flag) but if we saw any letters, they were of no interest to us at the time.

I remember my grandparents adding running water and an indoor bathroom when I was a boy. It was a typical family farmhouse surrounded by trees and plenty of space for kids to explore. My siblings, cousins, and I enjoyed exploring these woods and the surrounding area many times when we visited our grandparents. At the time it never crossed my mind that possibly our fathers had done the same.

My grandmother had a garden just north of the house and, among other things, I remember she had tall hollyhocks in the garden. In the

Dad (left) with brothers, Jim and Monroe, in front of a play house built by their maternal grandfather, 1928.

My grandparents in the back with their sons, Monroe (left), Jim (center), and Dad (right), ca. 1936.

front yard on the south side of the house, she also had a couple bushes of peonies and a lilac bush. An open front porch was a place to relax or play but was enclosed in the 1960s. The front of the house had two stained glass windows on the top one-third of the two largest windows. One of these stained glass windows now graces my house as it catches the morning sun.

Along with his brothers, Dad worked on the farm to take care of the chickens, pigs, cows, horses, and crops. There was also wood to cut and haul to the wood box inside the backdoor pantry. I'm sure farm life and the accompanying responsibility of daily chores contributed to the work ethic that was an important part of Dad's character and helped to shape how his life turned out.

School Days

Dad attended grades 1st through 4th in Fosston Public School, beginning first grade with Miss Ketten as his teacher on September 27, 1927. He attended part of 4th grade in International Falls but finished the school year in Fosston when the family moved back to that small town. With the move to the farm in 1931, Dad attended 5th grade at the Cheerful Nook School, a one-room country school about a mile

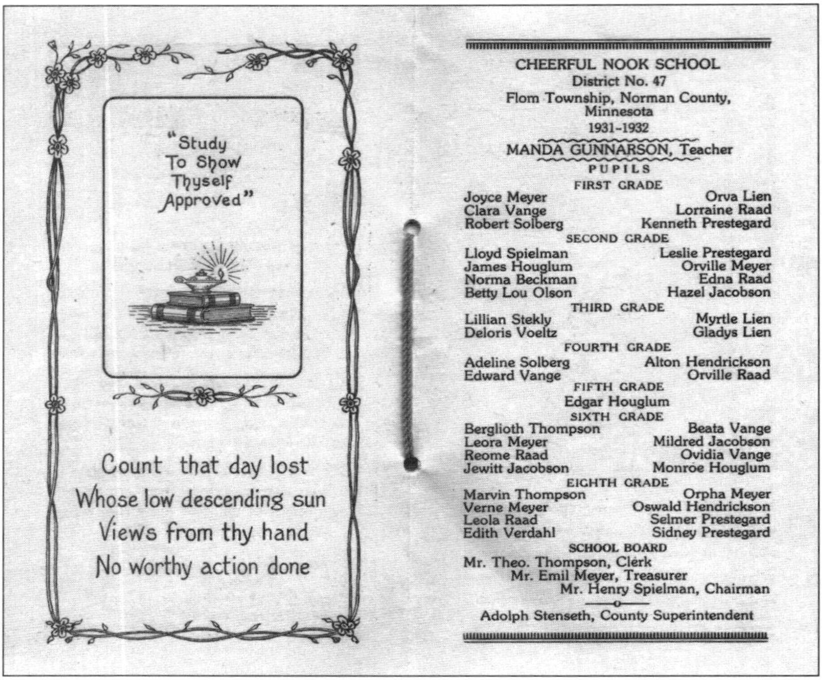

"Study To Show Thyself Approved"

Count that day lost
Whose low descending sun
Views from thy hand
No worthy action done

CHEERFUL NOOK SCHOOL
District No. 47
Flom Township, Norman County,
Minnesota
1931-1932
MANDA GUNNARSON, Teacher
PUPILS
FIRST GRADE
Joyce Meyer — Orva Lien
Clara Vange — Lorraine Raad
Robert Solberg — Kenneth Prestegard
SECOND GRADE
Lloyd Spielman — Leslie Prestegard
James Houglum — Orville Meyer
Norma Beckman — Edna Raad
Betty Lou Olson — Hazel Jacobson
THIRD GRADE
Lillian Stekly — Myrtle Lien
Deloris Voeltz — Gladys Lien
FOURTH GRADE
Adeline Solberg — Alton Hendrickson
Edward Vange — Orville Raad
FIFTH GRADE
Edgar Houglum
SIXTH GRADE
Berglioth Thompson — Beata Vange
Leora Meyer — Mildred Jacobson
Reome Raad — Ovidia Vange
Jewitt Jacobson — Monroe Houglum
EIGHTH GRADE
Marvin Thompson — Orpha Meyer
Verne Meyer — Oswald Hendrickson
Leola Raad — Selmer Prestegard
Edith Verdahl — Sidney Prestegard
SCHOOL BOARD
Mr. Theo. Thompson, Clerk
Mr. Emil Meyer, Treasurer
Mr. Henry Spielman, Chairman
Adolph Stenseth, County Superintendent

Center pages of the "Lest We Forget" pamphlet given by the school teacher to her pupils at Cheerful Nook country school, 1932.

north of the farm house. He was the only student in the 5th grade, which years later allowed him to jokingly claim on several occasions to be at the top of his class at Cheerful Nook. At the end of the school year in 5th grade, the teacher of Cheerful Nook, Miss Gunnarson, gave a souvenir pamphlet to all the pupils by which to remember the year. The title of the pamphlet was "Lest We Forget." It contained some quotes from Longfellow and others, and a list of pupils from each grade.

Dad's Norman County report cards for 5th–7th grades contain a section for good character, with grades for each of eight characteristics (obedience, orderliness, promptness, courtesy, industry, perseverance, cleanliness, attentiveness). Notably, Dad received the highest attainable grade for each character trait on each grade report. On June 24, 1935, Dad graduated from 8th grade in a joint ceremony of all 124 eighth grade students from all the Norman County country schools.

After the country school, Dad attended Waubun High School where he participated in football, basketball, and theater. In the Junior Class production of "The Gay Deception" he played the lead male role of Candler Stoll. He was also the president of his senior class. Dad was a very good student, obtaining mostly "A"s throughout school. In high school he excelled particularly in math, chemistry, and physics, earning an A in each of these classes on every report card, except for one B+ in the first six-week period as a freshman. Effort and conduct were always an A. There were thirty students in his graduating class on June 1, 1939.

Dad's high school graduation picture, 1939.

After High School

During the first year after graduation, Dad worked on a nearby farm for Bill Ommodt and took correspondence courses in bookkeeping, accounting, and business management from the American Technical Society located in Chicago, Illinois. On July 1, 1940, he began working at the Flom Co-operative Creamery. He worked there until September 20, 1942, when he started college at North Dakota Agricultural College in Fargo, North Dakota. Evidently his strong moral character and work ethic were notable while working in the creamery. Two years after Dad left the creamery, the manager of the creamery, Henry Ommodt, wrote a letter of recommendation for Dad when he was applying for the Air Corps. Mr. Ommodt said, *"I have known Pvt. Edgar Houglum for many years and have found him to be one of the finest young men that has left our Community… I wouldn't hesitate to recommend him to anyone as I am sure he will do his very best on any job he is put to do. He has a kind disposition good habits and a fine personality."* (February 22, 1944)

When the fall quarter began at North Dakota Agricultural College (NDAC) on September 24, 1942, Dad was a freshman with a mechanical engineering major. This choice for his major was a natural selection for Dad since when he lived on the farm, his talent for designing

Dad playing with hay wagon he made, ca. 1932.

Dad's homemade outdoor shower, ca. 1940.

and building things was evident. One such example was the toy horse-drawn hay wagon that he made as a boy. Another example was the outdoor shower he added onto the west side of the pump house. The western sun heated the water to provide a warm shower. This was not an elaborate or fancy addition, but Dad had an aptitude for designing and building mechanical things.

When Dad started college, he and his brother Jim were roommates in an apartment in Moorhead, the sister city of Fargo just across the Red River. Jim attended Moorhead State College while Dad attended NDAC. The move to Fargo-Moorhead area put Dad over fifty miles from the family farm, quite a distance in those days, but it would be the closest to home that he would live for the next five years. At NDAC, Dad also enrolled in the reserve officers training program (ROTC) and then on November 5th he enlisted in the army reserves. After two quarters and a 3.9 gpa, his college career at NDAC came to an end when he was called to report to active duty on April 5, 1943. His plans to become an engineer were put on hold to serve his country.

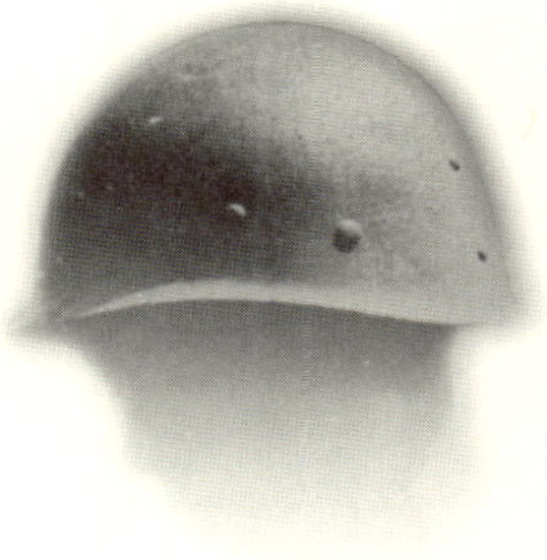

Chapter Three

In The Army Now

Dad's induction into the Army occurred at Fort Snelling in St. Paul, Minnesota. At that time his older brother Monroe was already in the Army (entering in 1942) and serving as a second lieutenant in "I" Battery, 85th Calvary, Newport News, Virginia. Having previously gone through the induction process, Monroe sent Dad a letter just days before he was due to report (postmarked March 29, 1943), and gave him some brotherly advice and encouragement.

Sunday Night

Dear Edgar,

So Uncle Sam wants another good man in the army? If this thing lasts long enough, Jim will probably have a chance to claim he's the last and the best of the Houglum's again – but I can't imagine a tough old seargent swallowing that on the day Jim is inducted. Here's hoping it's all over long before then.

Let's see – you'll get this just a day or two before you leave – at least you should.

The first thing that will happen to you will be a short interview – then a physical and when you get finger printed, you'll know that you're in. After that you'll raise your right hand and swear. After that you'll probably be one of a group of about 30 men known as ROSTER # ____ [blank in letter]. *You'll be led around and will live as a group. You'll be sold insurance – asked about War Bonds – you can buy them in amounts of $3.75, $6.25 etc. per month, the money to be deducted from your pay. Your Insurance will cost you about 65¢ per thousand* *per month. You'll take some tests – Mechanical Aptitude, Army I.Q., probably another. You'll be interviewed – if you've already taken your tests ask the boy who interviews you what you scored – the scores will be on your card upon which he is writing. Don't be too modest when you are being interviewed – ~~emphasize~~ Mention that you won letters in BB & Football was Class Pres – that card will tag you around wherever you go as an Enlisted man – and it's important in getting you into Service schools etc.*

The tests aren't particularly hard. Don't waste too much time on some thing you can't figure out - go on to the next – but don't skip too many. Use your imagination if you have to count blocks – picture in your mind what number each row contains and then just add them up – it's as easy as that.

After that you'll get a couple of shots and a vaccination. You may feel a little sick after 40 minutes or so – you'll get your clothing – if you're handed a pair of pants made of blanket like material, tell the boy they won't fit, maybe he'll give you a worsted pair.

Don't be in awe of any Sgts or officers you come in contact with. Nobody really knows anything in this army – you just pass the buck along – at least that's how it sometimes seems.

Do as you're told, and don't take yourself or anyone else too seriously.

If you're given any choice as to branch of the Service I'd ask for the Air Corps 1, Signal Corps 2, Medical 4, or Anti Aircraft 3, in about that order – for one reason – these branches have more service schools, where they send boys with brains.

Ft. Snelling is a nice place. Take advantage of free time – Post Theatre you get there by catching a street car behind the brick barracks north of the Reception center. You can ride down to Mpls or St. Paul by dropping a dime in the gadget by the conductor. You catch these cars where the Dummy line stops – opposite the main PX – As you face the PX, Mpls. cars run to ~~the~~ your left or West – St. Paul to your right or East. The Main drag in Mpls. is Hennepin Avenue – in St. Paul Wabasha Ave. The Service Club in Mpls. is over the State Theatre on Hennepin Ave and 8th St. maybe 7th St. In St. Paul it's on your right as you ride downtown – about where St. Peter Ave crosses 7th St.

Goodnight then, good luck, let's hear from you and I'll bet you'll like the Army better than you expect to right now.

Monroe

Fort Riley for Basic Training

Dad was only at Fort Snelling a short time (maybe a week) and was shipped to Fort Riley, Kansas, for basic training. On a post card from Dad to "Mom, Dad, & Jim" written at a stop over in the train depot in Kansas City, Dad wrote, *"Practically all you see around here is service men of one kind or another."* No doubt the train depot was a busy place with soldiers being shipped to various places across the country and other soldiers traveling to and from places on furloughs and passes. In several cards and letters, Dad and Monroe mentioned trying to make train connections to get to and from the farm and their military base. Sometimes they missed connections because of late trains; it seems quite similar to today's travel on air planes.

Another letter that Monroe sent to Dad, postmarked May 4, 1943, and sent to Dad's Fort Riley address revealed a little about life as a soldier in the states.

Monday Night

Dear Edgar,

How's soldiering? Ridden any horses yet?

This letter I'm answering is dated April 13, so I guess it's about time I'm answering. Your stay in Snelling wasn't too long but you seemed to make fairly good use of the time there.

I'm on a house cleaning spree tonight. Cleaning out my foot locker – getting my sun-tans out so I can get them pressed before we begin wearing them. By the way, if you ever need any clothing let me know and I'll get it for you at the Q.M. [quarter master].

My foot locker was a mess – still is for that matter.

I'm also cleaning out my letter box. I intended to catch up on my letter writing tonight but I'm discovering that I have too many letters. So I guess I'll just write you & Thelma tonight and catch up on the others tomorrow and later on.

Things have been popping around here lately. On Saturday the Colonel decided to visit and inspect. First time I've seen the "Old Man" since reporting to him last January. No, that's not quite true – He was down at Pendleton one night for one of our missions but I was too busy to say hello and he walked into Battalion Hq. one day when I was there. Anyway we all hustled like mad – some fun.

We've moved into the barracks now, and I'm in my hut – everything fair except that we have no running water – pretty unhandy. A pit latrine – 2 – 2x6's where you let fly and hope your aim was good and the channel not obstructed. Then when it rains we wade in mud – and when the sun comes out the mud becomes almost cement – a very peculiar type of clay soil. Still we have a small farm down on the east end of our position – better than an acre for our victory garden. I'm victory garden officer – got 8 of the damn things – didn't think I'd get into the Army to farm – my spring work is being held up however because I can't get seeds.

Over in K Btry when the last group of boys left for Texas for an overseas cadre, the remaining men in one of their light sections bought and put up in their window, a flag with 3 stars – 3 of their boys had gone to the Army.

Just looking over the pictures taken when I was home & before you left. You certainly look natural on that manure sled. Just like 3-4 years ago. Butch riding the pig is good too.

My Grandfather (left), Jim (center), and Dad (right) on manure sled referred to by Monroe in letter of May 4, 1943.

Listen soldier, why so secretive about what you're doing? Some special outfit?

Wouldn't I like to meet you now. See you salute and remember your "Sir" too.

I'm going to be looking for a long letter from you one of these days. If I don't get it, I'll make it an order that you write me once a week. How are your officers, your buddies, quarters, grub, passes etc. Maybe the Horse Cavalry is almost as good as the "Moonlight Cavalry." Let's hear about it. – what say?

Butch riding the pig referred to by Monroe in letter of May 4, 1943.

Good night then Edgar, and may the best of everything come your way.

Luck & Love,
Monroe

Dad must have responded to this letter of Monroe's with one that included the "sir" that Monroe lightheartedly mentioned, because in a letter to my Dad postmarked May 17th, Monroe put a "P.S." at the end of the letter saying, *"For the present we'll skip the sir."* After reading these and other letters from Monroe to my Dad, it appears that even though their army experiences were different, it provided some common topics of interest for them to stay connected through their letters. This shared experience eventually included the youngest of the three brothers, Jim.

The brothers, Monroe (left), Jim (center), and Edgar (right), 1946.

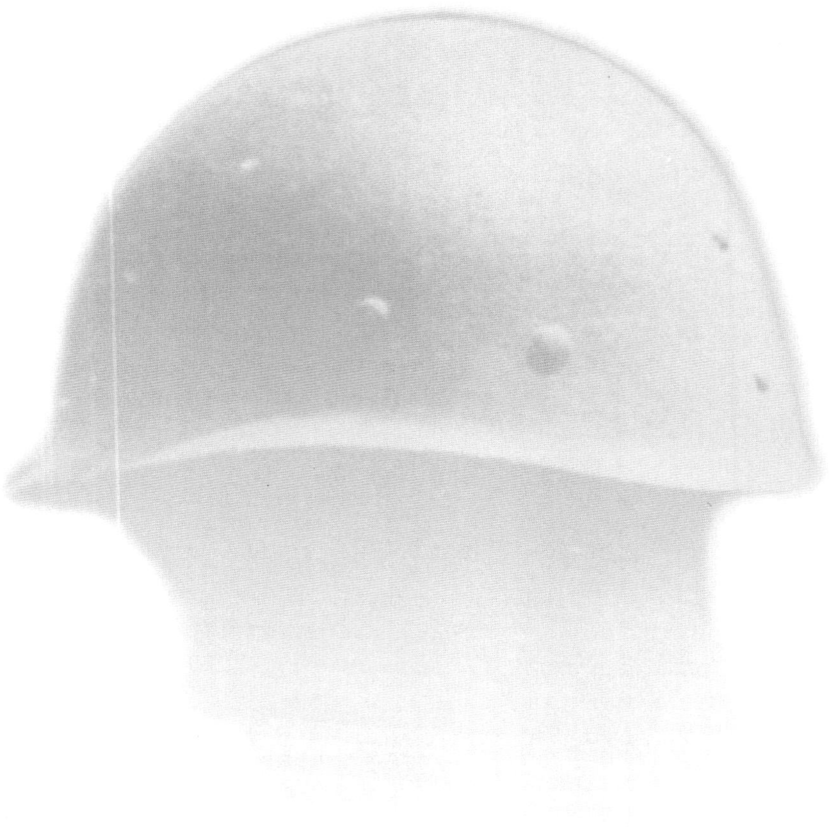

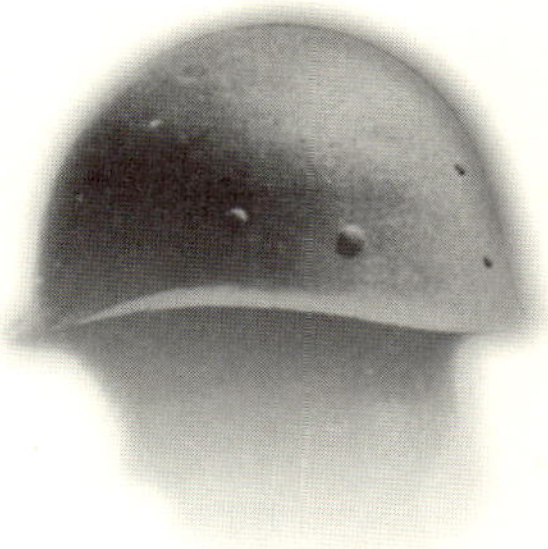

Chapter Four

You Got Mail

The importance of receiving news from home for soldiers hasn't changed since World War II . Our daughter, Cate, served in the Middle East just prior to and during the second Gulf War. She recalls that in spite of the existence of cell phones, text messages, and email at the time she was serving, there were many specific instances when mail call was quite memorable. She relates the following example of Easter Sunday:

We had been in country for about three to four months and we were completely isolated from EVERYONE and EVERYTHING for roughly two months at this point. Easter rolled around and we got "the day off" ... great. Day off meant nothing really. I can't express how isolated we were. Outside the berm in every direction you looked, for as far as the eye could see, was sand. Nothing but sand. I remember laying on my cot and talking to my platoon sergeant about what we were going to do. It was almost worse having the day off because there was nothing to do. It was kind of a let down. Everyone was thinking the same thing... what our families would be doing on that day without us. After we moved north I had only talked to my family once on the phone and considering holidays are a huge family day it was more depressing than I thought it would be, until the mail arrived. There was a stretch of about two to three weeks were I was receiving at least two packages everyday from my family and friends. I was a platoon leader at that time and I had about 40 men and women, but there was also roughly another 50 soldiers that at any given time were where we were at and it was common knowledge among everyone that if you needed something the odds were I had it sent to me already and everyone was welcome to anything they needed in those boxes. The mail arrived and I don't even remember what was in the box I got, except for a video tape my parents had made of them, my grandmother, and my church family sending me greeting. One of my squad leaders had a small 12" TV with a built in VCR that had seen more countries than I had at that point and we put the tape in. The first thing that came up was my parents sitting with my grandmother. I couldn't control my emotions at that point, and still today I have a hard time not tearing up thinking about that moment. It was obvious I needed some time so the few soldiers that were in the tent with me left and [I] *watched the video alone. Afterwards I played it again and pointed out some people to my platoon on the tape. "She's the one that baked the cookies, and I used to babysit their kids when they were little" "She sent the socks you needed, remember" and "These are my parents with my grandmother" who was holding the* [stuffed] *camel I had sent back to her. I think in that moment when we all watched the video together it was kind of a communal "hello, we are thinking of you" from everyone's family, and for me, it was an Easter I will never forget.*

[Note: Jim and Chris Adkins, family friends, had the video idea and recorded the video of our church congregation greeting Cate.]

Staying in the Loop

We do not have all of the letters that Dad received during the more than four years he was in the Army, but he saved over one hundred of them. There are some time periods when he received very few and others when he received many, such as May 1-17, 1943, when he received at least ten letters. While at Fort Riley, Kansas, Dad received letters from family, friends, and neighbors. I don't know how so many people got Dad's address; possibly my grandmother distributed it, but all his letters were addressed in virtually identical fashion:

Pvt. Edgar J. Houglum 17053907
Troop N, 4th Squadron
2nd Platoon, Bldg. 2704

C.R.T.C.
Fort Riley, Kansas

I'm sure news from home was always a morale booster, even if it meant having to write a response; maybe Dad enjoyed writing responses. Frequently the letters contained questions for Dad to answer, which probably gave him a good starting point in his response. Most letters were chit-chat about the things going on back home, the social calendar of the letter writer, the weather, or statements of encouragement. Receiving these letters must have been the "next best thing to being there" as a means for him to stay in the loop regarding the goings-on at home and in the lives of friends, former classmates, relatives, and neighbors.

Years later, when Dad was a rural mail carrier, I remember when I accompanied him on his mail route during the summer that as we drove up to the mail box sometimes one of the children from that family waited eagerly to receive the mail from Dad. He would place the mail in the youngster's hand and typically offer a tease like, "Are you playing hooky from your chores today?" If a parent was walking out to greet Dad, he would wait until the person got to the mailbox so he could say "hello," and if a young child was with him, Dad would say, "I see you have a helper today." I wonder if the eagerness he saw on the faces of children and adults alike reminded Dad of how important the mail was to him years earlier. I also wonder if one reason he enjoyed his job was because he knew how important it was to people to receive letters, cards, and packages. Maybe that is why he always made the extra effort to complete his route, even during snow storms.

Letters from Friends and Relatives

Donald Ommodt was the son of Henry who was the manager of the creamery in Flom (see Chapter 2). Donnie was a family friend, and even though he was a few years younger than Dad, Donnie was faithful to write several letters to Dad; this one when Dad was at Fort Riley.

Flom, Minn.
May 12, 1943

Dear Edgar,

I received that card of pictures you sent me. Thanks a lot. It must be a nice place were you are.

How do you like it there? Just fine I hope. I like it here.

... I am nailing butter boxes part part [sic] *of the time. They are using wooden boxes to send some of the butter in.*

... I was to the ball game Sunday. Flom and Mahnomen, 4 to 18 in favor of Flom. You should have been 1st base man then they wouldn't have got any points.

I got a airplane to put together. But I don't know how to cut out the wooden peices (please answer this.) Tell me how to do this when you write.

We just had company. Helen Jean and her girl friend Norma Beckman so it got so late. I will finish your letter tomorrow.

(Next Day)

Mother and Daddy has been to Ada today. Mother broght me a cardboard Army Battery set. With 18 figh[t]*ing men, Troop Truck, Mobile Gun, Motorcycle signal man. I had to punch it out and then fold it together. I just finish it and it sure looks pretty.*

We haven't played much croquet yet. It's been so cold in the evenings. Sure wish you could be here to play with us.

... Mother is serving Ladies Aid on Friday. She said I should greet you from Her and Daddy

Your pal,
Donald

Write me a long, fat letter.
Send some more pictures
I'll write again soon.

Among the other letters Dad received at Fort Riley was one from Bette and Shirley Jesness. They were Dad's younger cousins; Dad's mother and the girls' father were siblings. He received several letters from these girls while in the Army. I'm sure it was a delight for Dad to

Dad's cousins, Shirley and Bette Jesness, April 1944.

Dad and family friend, Donald Ommodt, September 1942.

hear from these younger cousins, and they seemed to enjoy writing to him. In 1943 Bette was twelve years old and wrote to Dad.

408 – 8th Street
Minneapolis
May 16, 1943
[Sunday]

Dear Edgar,

We got your letter Friday. You sure went places fast, didn't you. Did you travel by train way down there?

We were wondering why we didn't hear from you. We thought maybe you had lost the address.

I noticed the stationary you wrote on. Did they give it to you? Or did you buy it?

Say you said something about the weather there. Boy, you should be here. I've never seen such awful weather. It seems like its raining all the time. Yesterday it rained a stedy streak. It looks like it's going to clear up today. If it gets nice we're going on a picnic. There is going to be a parade here today, because today is "I Am An American" Day.

If you see a lot of mistakes just agnore them. I haven't an earaser, and if the writing is crocked just ignore that too, because I'm laying on the bed writing this. Shirley is writing to some kids at Bagley and mom is studying.

Yesterday I wrote to Buck Taylor. He's a guy I know that is over in New Guinea. I've gotton three letters from [him] *one was from California, one was from Austrailia & my last one was from New Guinea.*

Say, a week ago last Friday we had a Test Blackout. We were uptown and was it ever fun to watch all the lights go out. Guess I'll close now.

Love,
Bette

P.S. Mom will be writing soon.

A couple items in Bette's letter are of particular interest from a historical perspective. One is the test blackout in Minneapolis, a sight that will not likely be ever observed again. The other is the mention of "I Am An American Day." The designation of the third Sunday in May each year to be nationally celebrated as "I Am An American Day" was initiated in 1940 to recognize all who were born or naturalized as citizens of the United States. The civil and educational authorities were urged to observe the day. In 1952, Congress moved the date to September 17th to commemorate the signing of the Constitution of the United States and the designation was changed to "Citizenship Day." In 2004, Congress changed the designation to "Constitution Day and Citizenship Day" and added the directive that each year on this occasion each federal employee be given information regarding the Constitution and that every educational institution receiving federal funding provide a program on the Constitution for its students. So, over the years, not only did the date of observance change, but the focus was changed from a parade-like celebration of United States citizenship, to an educational observance of the Constitution.

A Fourth of July greeting card sent to Dad from his brother, Jim on July 1, 1943. This is a Forget-Me-Not greeting card.

During the World War II era, the incentive and enthusiasm for displays of patriotism was heightened and was the impetus for the public to demonstrate patriotism through a public parade and flag waving. I'm not sure fanning the patriotic flame through such events ever grows old. When soldiers returned from the Gulf wars, parades for the returning soldiers in many towns and cities across the country also sparked patriotism.

On July 1st, Dad's younger brother, Jim, sent a "A Big Hello To My Brother In the Service" greeting card to Dad at Fr. Riley and wrote a short note on the back.

Twin Valley, Minn.
July 1, 1943

Dear Edgar,

I just finished breakfast – but we have milked. I should be out in the corn field but it looks like rain again and its wet enough, too – so I'm no hurry.

Yesterday after lunch we stacked some alfalfa – and was it green. Pa says it's the best hay he's ever cut. But it don't get a chance to dry.

Greetings to a Ruth Carlson – she's O.K. Too bad she's so far away.

Butch [their dog] *is sitting here whining – he wants to go out. He sits on the tractor and is in the way all day. I guess Ma told you about my getting stuck – and I do mean stuck. I figure on going to the fair Sunday – well I'm out of space.*

Jimmy

Spiritual Encouragement

Mrs. Theo A. Thompson was a friend and neighbor who lived about a mile or so northeast of the farm. The Thompsons had a son, Marvin, who was also in the service. My Uncle Jim remembers that when he was a young boy he walked to the Thompson farm with my grandmother when she wanted to have coffee and talk with Thora. In a letter written to Dad, dated May 13th, Thora said, *"you know your Mom is just like a sister to me. At least that's the way I feel about her anyhow."* In two letters that Thora sent to Dad at Fort Riley, she gave Dad spiritual encouragement. In her May 13th letter she said,

> *And here's hoping this letter will find you in the best of health & full of spirit and courage. And also put your Trust to the Lord Edgar and all will be well. No matter how dark the cloud may be there will always be a ray of sunshine.*

Each time I read Thora's letters I am blessed that she would write such encouragement to my Dad, especially this letter of May 2nd.

> *May 2, 1943*
> [Sunday]
>
> *Friend Edgar,*
>
> *Well today surely has been a long and dreary day. And then your thoughts will always wonder to old friends. So here goes a few words on a piece of lifeless paper so you can see we still think of you even thou you are many miles away. Well how does this knew life agree with you? Hope you are O.K. and like it. We where to church this morning and the rest of the day been just hanging around doing nothing. Well this last week it has been rainy and cold. So the field work dont get done very fast. Today it has been awful cold it dont warm up very fast. How's the climate where you are? I havent heard from Marvin for awhile now of course you know how we mothers are. Even if it aint long we think it is (ha). But there's one thing we mothers are with you all the way Edgar I expect you will laugh when you read my letter but perhaps that might do good. I would like to be a mouse in the corner when you read it (ha ha). This is my third letter this evening. And I still have Mar-*

Envelope used by Thora Thompson to mail a letter to Dad that she wrote May 2, 1943.

vin to write to. I try and write him 2 or 3 letters a week. Last time he wrote he had gotten 5 letters from me at one time So he had something to read then for awhile. Well Edgar I know this adventure you are taking is not a very easy one. But by trusting in the Lord he will carry you thru my boy. And when things look the darkest read the 91st Psalm there's quite a comfort in that. I dont mean to preach to you Edgar but thats what came to my mind so had to put it on paper to you. Here's hoping this letter will find you in the best of health & full of spirit & courage. As it takes a lot of courage now days no matter what we are at. Love to you from us all. If you can find time drop us a few words shall try and do my best in answering.

Thora

Among Dad's military effects was his pocket New Testament and Psalms. It has a brown cover and has seen some wear, so presumably Dad carried it on the battlefield. Stamped on the inside cover is the name of a chaplain at Fort Snelling, Alfred P. Kausler. The first pages of the New Testament contain a picture of the American Flag and a message from Franklin D. Roosevelt dated January 25, 1941 and says in part, *"As Commander-in-Chief I take pleasure in commending the reading of the Bible to all who serve in the armed forces of the United States."*

It is difficult to imagine a time of greater need for spiritual encouragement than the battlefield. Whether that spiritual encouragement came from letters written by people like Thora Thompson, the pocket New Testament, or praying with a buddy in a foxhole, the spiritual components of Dad's life must have aided him to get from one day to the next.

Also among Dad's effects was a prayer that years after the war he had written and used at Memorial Day gravesite services conducted by local veterans. In the prayer Dad refers to the departed soldiers as having now met *"Jesus, The Supreme Commander and Chief."* Unfortunately, that meeting would come too soon on French and German soil for many soldiers training with Dad at Fort Riley.

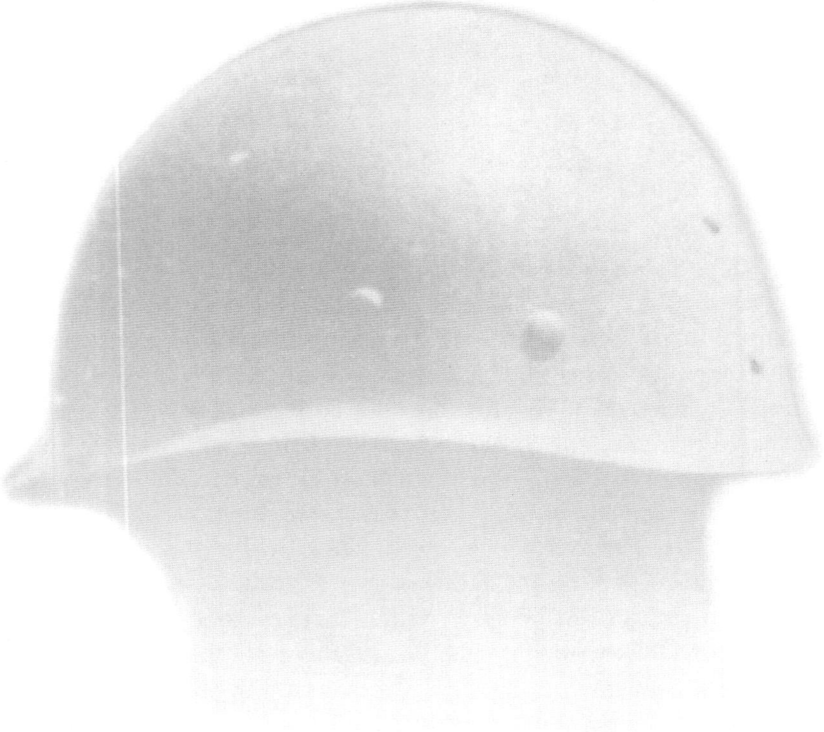

Chapter Five

Back To School: ASTP Training

Training at Fort Riley continued into July. On August 1, 1944, Dad entered the Army Specialized Training Program at the Missouri School of Mines in Rolla, Missouri. This was a program the Army was just starting. Soldiers were selected for ASTP primarily based on their Army General Classification Test score, high school diploma, and completion of some college courses in some cases. All candidates were enlisted men who had completed basic training. No doubt Dad's good grades in high school, his courses at NDAC, and the advice of his brother before he took the AGCT were helpful. In anticipation of needing well trained medical personnel and engineers, ASTP was the Army's program to quickly train these men.

The AST Program enrolled over 200,000 soldiers at 227 colleges, with a peak at any one time of 140,000. These men took accelerated courses for training primarily in the medical and engineering fields. It required these men to be full-time students but also full-time soldiers. They were required to have rigorous classroom instruction and military training during a standard work week of fifty-nine hours. In our Nation's history this unique program was only used during World War II. According to a report to a Congressional investigating committee in January 1944, ASTP was more demanding than either West Point or the Naval Academy.[1]

ASTP at Rolla

Class for ASTP in Rolla, Missouri, didn't start until August 9th, so Dad had a few days to acquaint himself with the campus and with Rolla, although judging from his postcards his exploration of the city was limited because he couldn't afford it. Nonetheless, he was enthusiastic about what the campus had to offer. Dad obtained some USO postcards that were free to service men, and also some picture postcards with pictures of the University of Missouri campus buildings. Apparently Dad really made use of these postcards because he sent no less than ten of them just to family members during the fall alone.

8-3-43

Dear Mom, Dad, & Jim,

Here's another card – picture of our U.S.O. here. Pretty nice building inside too.

Had a chance for a 3 day pass today, but am still broke so I had to let it go. Wasn't any place I could go anyway I guess. Meals are good here too, get a full quart of milk a day. Tonight we had steak and pie. They have quite an athletic schedule set up for us. Have to learn to swim I guess, which is O.K. by me. Darn nice pool to learn in anyway. Got sunburned today playing basketball – maybe I'll get a tan yet. Everything swell but the mail – haven't had any for over a week should get some soon. Goodnight.

Love,
Edgar

8-3-43

Dear Mom, Dad, & Jim,

Just a card tonight. Boy, this isn't the army. I'm pretty pooped tonight but its from play not work. Been playing basketball & swimming in the indoor pool practically all day. This morning we turned in some of our equipment we won't be using – gas mask, mess kit, helmet liner & overshoes. These are most of the buildings on the campus [postcard has 8 small pictures of campus buildings]. *The gym is over our barrack house & just to the left of the athletic field. Tennis court and basketball in the rear of gym. There are more trees than there are shown here. No more room.*

Love,
Edgar

Sun. Night
[postmarked August 10, 1943]

Dear Mom, Dad, & Jim,

I think I've got a few minutes left before lights out so I'll write a line. I picked up ½ doz. of these cards at the USO tonight. Got your letter today – thanks a lot. The boys are coming back from their passes. Lee & I have been going to shows to spend the time yesterday & today. Last night we saw a double feature – "Over My Dead Body" with Milton Berle, & "Truck Busters." Today "DuBarry was a Lady" with Red Skelton, Lucille Ball & Tommy Dorsey & his orchestra. Jim would have liked the drum solo & other numbers. Out of room. Goodnight. Love, Edgar.

Didn't see this! – extra space. Well, tomorrow the grind starts. Time should go pretty fast if we're kept busy and I guess we will be. Pictures turned out good – I'll send them on to Monroe when I write. Bette sure has grown. Plane looked pretty nice, too. Must have been some tornado.

That's all -
Edgar

[Note: This was the first of the USO postcards Dad used and was written on August 8th. After he had signed off he discovered that since there was no picture, there was space to write on both sides of the postcard: "Didn't see this!" There is no explanation in other letters as to what the "plane" and "tornado" were referring.]

The ASTP was a great opportunity for Dad to continue his study of engineering that he began at NDAC. His class schedule for the first three-month term which ended October 30, 1943, included physics,

English, history, drawing, geography, math, military, and physical education. Of course he continued to receive letters during this term; one was from a friend who also was evidently from Minnesota and had been at the Combat Readiness Training Center (CRTC) at Fr. Riley. Dad's friend was in the ASTP but located at South Dakota State College in Brookings (now South Dakota State University). Considering I was on the faculty at SDSU for nearly thirty years, this was of special interest to me. The letter was from Cadet Blake and postmarked August 31, 1943.

Monday

Dear Houglum & Co.,

I guess it's about time I drop you a line for I have been here about two weeks now. Just a little bit south of North Dakota. I bet you guys wouldn't mind being here with No Dak & Minn. so close.

I am 200 miles south of ~~Bisma~~ Fargo and about 400 miles from home. We cant get furloughs- but I am planning for a three day pass for home this weekend.

Our classes don't start until Sept. 13 but in the meantime we take a physical Ed program and I do mean physical fitness we hike more here than back in the darn C.R.T.C. – almost.

As things look now we will have a pretty good setup. We have rooms that are really super. Two to a room with built in bunks and desks around the walls. Inner spring mattress and a wash sink in every room.

The city of Brookings isn't quite what it should be for entertaining soldiers, but once college starts they should have a few coeds around.

The only guy from C.R.T.C. with me here is Hugh Fisher of 2705. He is from Georgia and will have a nice time this winter – right?

Well I hope your studies aren't too hard so try and sneak in an answer to this half way letter.

Bye now, DB

Cadet Donavon Blake 17053873
Co. B. A.S.T.U. # 3707
Wecota Annex, Brookings So. Dak.

In her autobiography, *The Winds of Change,* former dean of women at SDSU, Vivian V. Volstorff states, *"I shall never forget the arrival of the very first army unit one morning at about 5:30 a.m. at Wecota Cafeteria. Every window in Wecota and Wenona* [University dormitories] *had girls looking out wondering what it would mean in their lives to have the army living in Wecota Annex. The army was elated to be served real eggs instead of dried ones for that first breakfast at State."*[2]

On September 8, 1943, the surrender of Italy was announced by General Eisenhower, and at noon on that same day Dad took time to write home on one of the USO postcards, *"We just heard the good news from across the pond of Italy's surrender. They're sure doing O.K. Some of the boys are already talking of getting their discharge, packing their barracks bags etc. Would be great, but I'm afraid it isn't quite over yet. There goes school call so 'bye now, Love, Edgar."*

Another of these postcards reveals the stress of college final exams. This was postmarked two days before the end of his first term in ASTP, after which he was heading home for about a week on furlough.

Thurs. Noon
[postmarked October 28, 1943]

Dear Mom, Dad, & Jim,

Don't know if this card will beat me or not, but I'll write it anyway. We had a pretty stiff physics test this morning, so I don't know how I'll come out. Our geography wasn't too bad yesterday – no results out yet. This afternoon we have some kind of military test. Tomorrow morning, history & after dinner Math. Hist. might be kind of tough, but I've got an E to fall back on – same in Math. Sat Morning Eng – which I don't think will be a push over either.

Perfect day, today – hope it lasts.

Be seeing you soon, I hope.

Love,
Edgar

Visits Home

Most likely Dad was very busy helping with farm chores and visiting friends, neighbors, and relatives while he was on furlough. Portions of a couple letters from his brother, letting Dad know about Monroe's time at home during furlough, reveal how busy the time at home was likely to also have been for Dad.

Friday PM
[postmarked September 18, 1943]

Dear Edgar,

Got your Tuesday Night's letter this morning. I'm sorry to hear you can't get down.

I've been thinking of checking train schedules when we go to Fargo on Monday and see if I can work out going by way of St. Louis and Rolla on the way back to Virginia. I'll have to leave here either Wednesday or Thursday. I'll let you know what I find out.

Went to Ada [about 30 miles from farm] *this morning. Dad sold his wheat and flax – Got $500+ – Thelma renewed her Teacher's certificate, I got 5 gallons of gasoline – that is, a coupon for 5 gals. And Jimmy tried to get an inner tube for his bicycle tire.*

Wednesday we threshed. I shoveled grain. Thursday I woke up with a cold and sore back. Last night we went to Mahnomen [about 15 miles from farm]. *Thelma wanted to see Janice. She's teaching first grade there this year…*

Tonight Jim says there is a dance in Voss. Don't know whether we can stretch the gas or not.

Yesterday I plowed while Jim got the cows. Couldn't get the plow out of the ground at the end and clipped off part of an old fence post before I got the tractor around. Then I had to unhook the darn thing & back into the plow to pull that out. Think I'll let Jimmy do the plowing. Dad's cutting corn & Mom's washing clothes.

Think I'll go over & see Uncle Joe this afternoon – in the old puddle jumper – it's got both an A & B book.

By the time you get through with your school OCS should be a breeze academically – and the rest just demands an active sense of humor.

By the way the picture of you looks pretty sharp. Pretty good-looking soldier.

Here's hoping I'll see you then.

Love, Monroe

My new address will be,
328 AAA S/L Bn
Newport News, Va

Love,
Monroe

[Note: Janice was a friend of Thelma's. The "A&B" book refers to stickers that were used to enforce gas rationing that was initiated to save rubber. An "A" sticker allowed the person to purchase four gallons of gas per week and was issued to most everyone with a vehicle; a "B" sticker provided eight gallons per week and was issued to war workers; a "C" sticker was for doctors and other vital occupations; "T" stickers were for truckers. Typical highway speed limit was 35 mph.]

Sunday Morning
[postmarked September 26, 1943]

Dear Edgar,

Back in Virginia. Got into Suffolk this morning. Got a hotel room so I could clean up, maybe sleep a little and then after cleaning up I decided to write some letters.

It was pretty nice to be home again but every leave is always spoiled because you have to go back again.

We got home on Wednesday morning – slept for a few hours and then got up to find the threshers there. Threshing took care of Wednesday. Thursday we stayed around home in the morning and went over to Otterson's in the afternoon. Friday we went to Ada – stayed at home playing the phonograph and went to Mahnomen for a movie at night. On Saturday we went to Flom – saw Mrs. John Jacobsen, Nels, Clara, Henry Ommodt, who sends you greetings – Mabel – who sends more greetings – Andrew Anker – hello again – John Dorseth, John Haroldson, Mrs. Thorstenson, Oscar Morck, Kenny Engebritson, etc. At night Mom, Dad, Thelma & I went to show in Ulen – wild western – Saw Jim there but he had something else on his mind so he couldn't come home with us.

Sunday we went to see Hildur & the girls. Monday Thelma, Jim & I went to Fargo – Jim chased all over looked for a bicycle tube and records – he got 3 new records.

On Tuesday we went to Fosston – saw Mutt, Sheila, Nora, Roddy & Sel– Wednesday – we were over to Ottersons for a while – then to Thora's – saw Olaf & Knute Verdahl too – Olaf gave a pretty good summary of what had happened in his place in about 3 minutes of rapid talking. Still quite an Olaf. On Thursday we went to Waubun, saw Hemmelgarn's, Johnsons, Danielson's, Patnodes, etc. & stopped at Bill Ommodts on the way home. Saw Nolda & Arla but Bill was filling silo at Solbergs. Nolda had just received a letter from you – she's getting to be quite a girl. Left home on the flyer out of Waubun on Thursday night, hoping to be able to make connections & get to see you but couldn't do it. Just one train a day out of the cities to St. Louis – leaving at 5 P.M. – got to Chicago a little late. Had 4 hour waits at Mpls., Chicago, & Cincin[n]*ati… so if schedules hadn't have been so lousy I'd have seen you – maybe will when we move west – I hope.*

Love & write,
Monroe

[Note: Hildur was my grandfather's sister-in-law; Bette and Shirley were her daughters. At this time they lived in Park Rapids, about fifty-five miles southeast of my grandparents' farm. Mutt was my grandmother's brother, Sheila and Roddy were Mutt and Nora's children, and Sel (Selvina) was another of my grandmother's sisters-in-law. Fosston was about forty-five miles north of the farm. Henry and Bill Ommodt were brothers for whom Dad had worked in the creamery and on the farm, as mentioned in Chapter 2. Donald (not mentioned here) and Arla were the son and daughter of Henry and of Bill, respectively, and they both wrote letters to Dad. The other people mentioned were additional friends and neighbors.]

No doubt Dad's visits home were as busy as the ones Monroe described. There was plenty of work to do on the farm but also there were many friends, neighbors, and family that appreciated a visit from these soldiers. Considering my grandparents did not have a telephone, the sons' visits home probably also gave my grandmother a means of staying connected with neighbors and relatives. My grandparents were likely just as eager to see their sons as the sons were to be home. After all, with a world war raging the thought had to be looming as to whether this would be their last visit.

The following is a postcard Dad wrote the day after arriving back to Rolla after a one-week visit home between terms. He commented that it didn't seem like he was home, but only a dream.

Mon. Noon
[postmarked November 8, 1943]

Dear Mom, Dad, & Jim,

Back in the groove again – almost. Colder than heck down here – feels every bit as cold as it was there. Trying to snow this morning. Snowed and rained all the way down Sat. & yesterday. Had quite a bit all the way from Wadena to Minneapolis. We had to have our tickets changed in St. Paul. Didn't take long but long enough so we missed one of the trains. Caught another a little later and went by way of Chicago. Had breakfast there yesterday morning. Now that I'm back it doesn't seem that I ever was home – just like a dream. School call so that's all.

Love,
Edgar

Christmas 1943

The second term in ASTP ran from November 8, 1943, to the end of January 1944, and was more of the same course topics as the first term except for the addition of Mechanical and Power Trans(missions). Dad was not home for Christmas in 1943. He did receive Christmas cards from several friends and relatives; most did not have any message written with them. The Christmas card from his parents was specifically for a son in the service. Grandma did include

Christmas card sent to Dad from his parents, 1943.

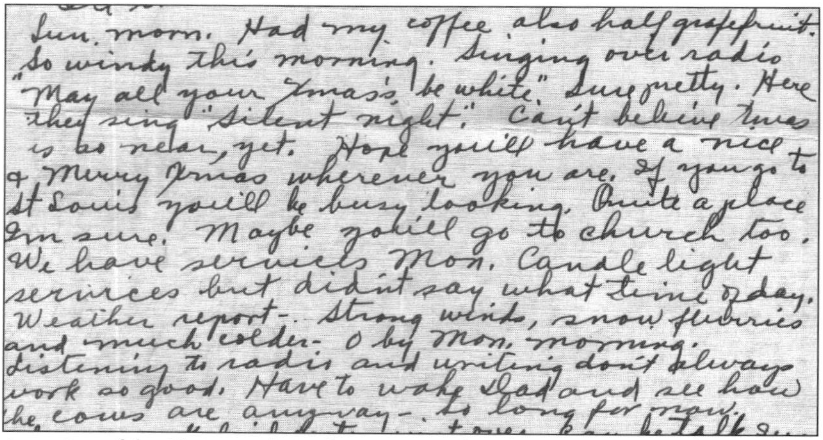
Sun. morn. Had my coffee also half grapefruit.
So windy this morning. Singing over radio
"May all your Xmas's be white" Sure pretty. Here
they sing "Silent night". Can't believe Xmas
is so near, yet. Hope you'll have a nice
& Merry Xmas wherever you are. If you go to
St Louis you'll be busy looking. Quite a place
Im sure. Maybe you'll go to church too.
We have services Mon. Candle light
services but didnt say what time of day.
Weather report- Strong winds, snow flurries
and much colder- O by Mon. morning.
Listening to radio and writing don't always
work so good. Have to wake Dad and see how
the cows are anyway- So long for now.

A portion of the Christmas letter from my grandmother that was included in the Christmas card, 1943.

a long letter (of course), which told of the usual happening around the area and included a Christmas wish.

[postmarked December 20, 1943]

Dear Edgar,

... Sun. Morn. Had my coffee also half grapefruit. So windy this morning. Singing over radio "May all your Xmas's be white." Sure pretty. Here they sing "Silent night." Can't believe Xmas is so near, yet. Hope you'll have a nice & Merry Xmas wherever you are. If you go to St Louis you'll be busy looking. Quite a place Im sure. Maybe you'll go to church too. We have services Mon. Candle light services but didn't say what time of day. Weather report - Strong winds, snow flurries and much colder - O by Mon. morning. Listening to radio and writing don't always work so good. Have to wake Dad and see how the cows are anyway - So long for now.

... Xmas program at Aspelund tonite. The Meyer children are sick, so they are home. Merril B. was to be in the program but heard he didn't feel good today. So many can't give their part coz they're sick. Jim heard Rev. was sick too.

... Well this must do. We'll be thinking of you and you are at home, you are in U.S. Thank God.

Lots of luck & love –
Mom

[Note: Meyer children are neighbors and Merrill B. (Braaten) is Grandpa's nephew. My grandparents were members of a three-church parish of Aspelund, Wild Rice, and Emmanuel.]

After Christmas, Dad got a letter from his cousin Bette, thanking him for the money he sent for their Christmas presents.

December 30, 1943
Park Rapids, Minn.

Dear Edgar,

Thanks for the money you sent. Shirley and I took each others dollar and got each other something. I got Shirley a doll house and she got me bedroom slippers.

Monroe sent us some mittens each. White ones for Shirley, red ones for me, and orange ones for Mom. He also sent us some candy.

Did you get the package we sent you? We sent the same thing to Monroe. We sent ones to Floyd and Lloyd, only theirs said "Navy" on them, and were blue.

We went to Minneapolis for Xmas and stayed two days. We went on the bus. Shirley & I sure had fun. Although it was tiresome. We rode for 7 hours going and 7 hours coming back. We got there at 8 o'clock Christmas Eve, and went at 12 o'clock the day after Xmas day.

I got a pair of figure skates from Mom, pajamas, & a slip. Other presents I got were; two bottles of perfume, and "Evening In Paris" set, a ring, a "Tangee" set, a box of candy and etc. We (Shirley & I) bought a real pretty blouse for Mom. We had $5.00 saved up. We had a little bit left over so we got her a necklace and pin.

... I'm running out of news so guess I'll close now.

Your cousin,
Bette

[Note: Floyd and Lloyd were Bette's uncles; her mother's brothers. Minneapolis is about 210 miles southeast of Park Rapids.]

For soldiers away from home, knowing that people back home are thinking about them is a morale booster. Even the short note from Aunt Selvina Jesness, dated January 14, 1944, must have been encouraging as she ended it, *"Hope this finds you in good health, and remember we are thinking of you."* In some cases the letters were evidently from people whom Dad would not have expected to write. Here is a letter from Dad's Uncle Mutt (Martin); my grandmother's brother.

Feb 2 – 44

Hello Edgar,

Stunned! Eh? Knocked on your fanny I'll bet to see who is doing the writing. I was kind of flabbergasted myself to see that I could still write.

It's about time I do I guess. I'll have writers cramps maybe before I get the first page done. Sounds like I intend to write more than one page. That I won't bank on.

How's things going? Suppose your studying your head off. I don't know how tough engineering is but got a hunch its damn tough. Especially when you take it in such big doses in such a short time. Something like taking Exlax, thinking its candy.

Reminds me of something funny. When your Dad's brother lived in Montana, (think he is at International Falls now) he ran across a guy who was trying to invent a suspension bridge across the Missouri River. Concrete posts on each side of the river, with cables running across on which a platform traveled, pulled by a drum, driven by a gas engine. Kind of nuts. Your uncle must of seen something was wrong, but to satisfy this guy who was looking for someone to draw a plan, he gave him my name. I got a letter from this bird, with all the instructions. That is all he had anyway. I wrote back and got him to make a few things clearer. Next time he wrote me he put an M.E. [mechanical engineer] *after my name. Well I drew the darn thing and sent it to him C.O.D. Don't remember what I charged him but it wasn't much. Should of took him for 25.00 bucks but in them days I didn't know better. Well I was an ME. once anyway. Laugh that off. That bird is probably prowling around some nuthouse calling himself Edison now.*

Mutt continued to write a five-page letter, telling Dad about his night job, the good grades received by his daughter (Sheila), the Fosston basketball team, how bare the ground had been until after mid-January, how everyone else in the household (Nora, Sheila, Roddy) were sick during Christmas time. He elaborates on news of five Jesness brothers that were his nephews (Dad's cousins): "Tops" Clancy in Idaho with scarlet fever, "Snuss" Leland also out there, Frandall in Hawaii, Kenneth in Washington or Oregon, and Jerry in New York. He ended the letter with,

> *Been sitting here trying to think of something to write about. Damifican. Might as well call it off.*
>
> *So long,*
> *Mutt*

ASTP Ends

The courses for Dad's third term of ASTP were English, geography, history, internal combustion engines, math, military, physics, and physical education. The third term started in February 1944, and even though it started much the same as the other two terms with the similar heavy load of courses, it ended much differently. The U.S. Infantry was in need of soldiers, especially with the invasion of Europe being planned. The ASTP students had already gone through basic training and were the largest ready source of more men. Consequently, in February 1944, most of the ASTP students were informed that they would be transferred to infantry, airborne, and armored divisions that were scheduled to be shipped overseas later that year. Enrollment in ASTP courses was reduced to about 50,000, primarily comprised of personnel being trained for medical positions or in other advanced courses. I can't imagine the blow this news was to these soldiers, including Dad, since this was the second time his training as an engineer was terminated. Based on his grades on his transcript, Dad was obviously doing well academically; his ASTP transcript states, *"Designated for scholastic excellence during Term 2."*

It was at this time that Dad applied for the Army air corps as an aviation cadet. In a letter from Monroe (February 23, 1944), Monroe wrote,

> *As for your application for entrance into the Air Corps as a cadet—not a bad idea, if you think that you'd like to fly. I don't know how much weight a letter of recommendation from me, being your brother, and naturally prejudiced, would carry, but I will write one for you and you can use your own judgment as to the advisability of using it. I've been half considering the Air Corps myself for some time. Rather in a half joking, half teasing way I'll admit, but the idea has been in my mind. Thelma says nope, but I think that I can win her over, --if I can make up my own mind definitely. This outfit has kind of lost its appeal. I doubt very much whether it will go over seas at any time…*

Dad's application for aviation cadet training was processed through Fort Leonard Wood, Missouri. Along with his application, Dad obtained letters of recommendation from Henry Ommodt, manager of the Flom Creamery, and from three faculty members at the University of Missouri School of Mines. One department head in engineering commented that Dad's institutional rank was Superior and that he was *"a young man of pleasing personality, excellent character and moral worth; and in my judgment would perform fully as well in the Air Corps as he has in his classes here."* In a letter to Monroe, Dad stated that his application was accepted but the number of accepted applications exceeded the quota, and although Dad could apply again if additional positions opened, he was not among those selected this time for the Air Corps. In a letter from Monroe postmarked March 7th, he provided some solace for Dad by saying that *"a Sgt. here in the Battery - one of the top men…"* also did not get accepted.

Dad's time in ASTP ended on March 15, 1944. His transcript indicates "WP" (withdrew passing) for all the courses for the third term. At the end of the transcript is the following statement, "SEPARATED FOR THE CONVENIENCE OF THE GOVERNMENT."

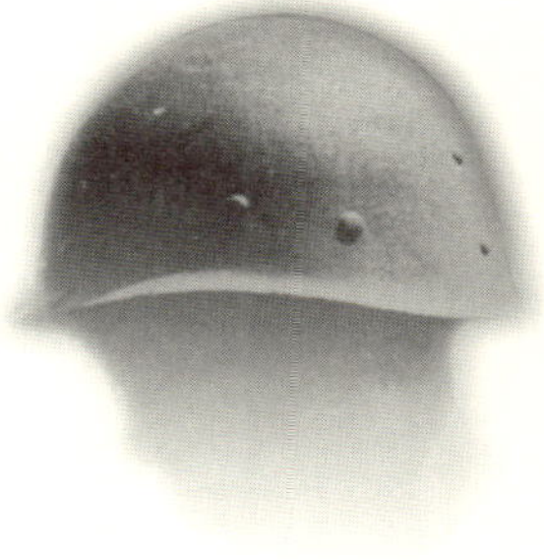

Chapter Six

Final Combat Training

Political support for the AST Program was not strong, thus there was no public or political outcry over the abrupt discontinuation of the program when the Army determined that the manpower needs in Europe were greater than anticipated. Even though the AST Program did not fulfill its intended mission of supplying highly trained personnel in specialized fields, a secondary benefit was that it brought male students to 227 land grant universities for a period of time after the ROTC programs had been suspended. When the Army disbanded the AST Program, the ASTP soldiers were distributed among thirty-five Army divisions.[1]

Dad was assigned to the 44th Infantry Division. The 44th was comprised of three regiments, 324th, 124th, and 71st Regiments. Dad was assigned to the 324th Regiment which had about 5,500 men (original plus replacements) who served in that regiment during World War II. The effective strength of the regiment varied with casualties and replacements, but on the first day of battle their effective strength of officers, support units, and men was 3,125, which translated to about 2,250 combat troops on the front lines.[3] Dad's regiment was comprised of three battalions (1st, 2nd, and 3rd) plus headquarters, anti-tank, cannon, and medical companies; Dad was in the First Battalion. Each battalion was comprised of four to five companies; Dad was in C "Charlie" Company but the three battalions of the 324th Regiment were comprised of companies A – M. About 400 men served in Company C during the war, but prior to combat the average per company was about 175 men. The companies were subdivided into platoons with 25 to 60 soldiers per platoon, lieutenants being the commanding officer of a platoon. Squads were smaller units of a platoon with 8 to 16 men in each.

Unit	Number of Men*	Made up of	Dad's Unit
Army Group	250,000	2+ armies	6th Army Group
Army	100,000	2-4 corps	Seventh Army
Corps	50,000	≥ 2 divisions	XV Corps
Division	12,000	2-4 regiments	44th Division
Regiment	2500	≥ 2 battalions	324th Regiment
Battalion	700	2-6 companies	First Battalion
Company	175	2-8 platoons	C Company
Platoon	50	≥ 2 squads	
Squad or Patrol	12		

*The numbers are approximate to provide a sense of the relative size of each unit but the number of men varies considerably from one specific unit to another of the same type. These numbers represent the unit size at full strength, a rare occurrence under combat conditions.

Camps Polk and Phillips

Dad left Rolla, Missouri, at about 5:15 p.m. on March 21, 1944, and was transported to Camp Polk, Louisiana, to join the 44th Infantry Division, 324th Regiment, First Battalion, Company C, which was on maneuvers in Louisiana. In route to Camp Polk, Dad wrote a short postcard home and said, *"Our destination is Camp Polk, Louisiana. Every thing O.K. Write more later. Love, Edgar."* Evidently he did not have much time to write once he arrived at Camp Polk. My grandmother must have been getting worried, especially considering Dad had been transferred to a whole new environment, with a new unit, and a completely different objective. In a long letter to Dad on April 2nd (Palm Sunday), tucked inside a "Happy Easter Son" card, my grandmother wrote,

> *Dear Edgar,*
>
> *Going to scribble some today too. Just wondering what you've been doing all week and when we'll hear from you*
>
> *... Had letters almost every day last week from Monroe or Thelma, but did we miss yours. Maybe won't be long before we hear from you now again.*

> *...Will be thinking of you and hoping Son*
> *Lots of luck & love,*
> *Jim, Dad & Mom*

Dad wasn't at Camp Polk long because in April 1944, the 44th Division, including the 324th Regiment, was transferred to Camp Phillips, Kansas, to complete their final overseas duty training. Dad must have eventually caught up with his letter writing because letters postmarked April 28th were addressed to Camp Phillips from his cousins, Shirley and Bette Jesness from Park Rapids, Minnesota. Evidently Dad had written to them and included birthday money for each of the girls. Bette thanked Dad for the money and mentioned that she was home with the German measles and that her mother was working at the "Enterprise" (newspaper) but *"can't make over $14.99 this month because then she'd have to send her social security check back..."* Shirley thanked Dad for the birthday money and told him that she was in the process of making May baskets, *"are they ever nice ones."*

Both Dad and his brother, Monroe, were planning furloughs that were evidently overlapping so that they could be home at the same time in June. In anticipation of the occasion, my grandmother's sister-in-law, Hildur Jesness, wrote to my grandparents on Sunday, June 12th. Hildur began the four-page letter with the salutation, *"Dearest Alma, Ed and James,"* and when referring to Dad and Monroe's visit home she said, *"glad to hear boys are coming home on furloughs. Yes, we sure want to see them – Maybe you could come here? If it's after the 20th I'll have gas too but not until then."* Gas rationing during World War II put a crimp on some family gatherings. Interestingly, in the same letter from Hildur, she gave another indication of the economic times and quality of life in 1944 as she wrote,

Dad with his parents before he "went across" in 1944.

I bought a second-handed ice-box at a community auction sale yesterday. Pd. $5.00 for it. Will give it a coat of enamel both inside and out and I think it will serve the purpose. Our butter has been so soft and milk sours so fast I had to get something. Girls [Bette and Shirley] *don't like milk and butter that way.*

Dad obtained his ten-day leave but Monroe did not; in fact, on August 6th Monroe wrote that he was *"still waiting for that long-promised leave."* Whether Dad visited his Aunt Hildur and cousins, Shirley and Bette, on his leave is not evident in his letters. On Friday, June 30th at 9:40 a.m. Dad wrote a postcard on his way back to Camp Phillips after his furlough. His coveted time at home must have evaporated quickly, and as he had stated in a previous letter, it was *"like a dream."*

Dear Mom, Dad, & Jim,

From Minneapolis. Got in about 8. Train leaves at 10:40. Stopped both in Wadena and Sauk Center. Had a pretty good ride although the road seemed unusually rough in spots to be pavement. Had supper and took a little walk across the bridge and back. As yet I haven't seen any of the other fellows. Already even 10 days seem like a dream. Guess I'm out of space. Might write from K.C.

Love,
Edgar

For Dad to get to Camp Phillips from the farm, someone had to drive him to Detroit Lakes (about thirty-five miles south) where he took the bus to Minneapolis, and then the train to Kansas City, switched trains to go to Salina, Kansas, and then caught a ride to Camp Phillips, located twelve miles southwest of Salina. In route back to camp after his furlough, Dad wrote from Kansas City another postcard at 4:45 p.m.

Dear Mom, Dad, & Jim,

This time from Kansas City. Train was about 2 hours late so didn't get in until almost 4:00. Right now I'm at a restaurant waiting for a meal. Slept most of the way from Minneapolis, not too comfortable but managed. Guess I'll have hamburger steak for supper. Train leaves at 6:30, which gives me an hour from Salina to camp if on time.

Love,
Edgar

Throughout August, the 44th Division finished their final overseas duty training at Camp Phillips. On August 17th, along with thirty-eight other members of the 324th Regiment, Dad was awarded the Expert Infantry Badge. Later that month the 44th Division left Camp Phillips for Boston, their port of departure for combat.

During the few days the 44th was in Boston they earned a reputation as the "fighting 44th." According to the website for the 44th Division,[4] soldiers from the 44th were involved in so many fights, drunkenness, and brawls that the mayor of Boston closed the bars and had all the soldiers removed from the city. General Spragins then banned the soldiers of the 44th from entering Boston. Although I am sure my Dad was not among that rowdy group of soldiers, for some of these men it would be their last night on the town.

Other Observations

It is difficult to comprehend the sacrifice endured by American soldiers and families of soldiers during World War II. Beyond these, many other Americans also made sacrifices during the war. One such group of people was the families that had to vacate their homes and land in 1942 for the construction of Camp Phillips. The Army needed additional training facilities and since Salina was near the geographic center of the United States, it was a convenient location to ship soldiers to the Atlantic or Pacific. The state of emergency gave the government authority to condemn the 45,000 acres of land and purchase it at reduced market prices. This land provided the space to construct 3,200 buildings to accommodate the training of 45,000 troops at any one time. Over a hundred farm families had to hurriedly sell their farms, livestock, and equipment and find other living quarters, even though some of these families had occupied the land for three or four generations.[5] This is another example of the sacrifice that folks of that generation endured so future generations could enjoy freedom.

One of the interesting observations from reading letters of this era is to discover that many of the aspects of daily life are similar to today. For example, the concern about getting off one train to make connections on another train is similar to today's busy society, but today it usually involves plane connections rather than train connections. Staying connected with family and friends today involves email and text messaging; staying connected was just as important in 1944, but it occurred by writing letters almost daily.

The 21st Century society does not have exclusive claim to constantly being on-the-go either. On several occasions people who wrote to Dad mentioned being too busy to write. As an example, Lois Ann Meyer (probably 7th or 8th grade student), who lived near the Houglum farm, wrote to Dad on May 2nd, *"Dear Edgar, I am taking off time in school to write you as I just haven't time any other time as I'm on the go every minute."* Evidently she had sent Dad a copy of the Cheerful Nook school news, "Cheerful Highlights," and Dad had written to Lois to thank her. Not only did the school news keep Dad connected to his home area, but so did Lois' letter as she continued her letter, *"I am glad you like the Cheerful Highlights and was glad to hear you had received it. Now for the news around here."* Lois went on to describe who she was visiting and who was visiting her, what social gatherings she was attending, and, of course, the weather. This was the email and text messaging of 1944, and I can imagine it made Dad feel closer to home.

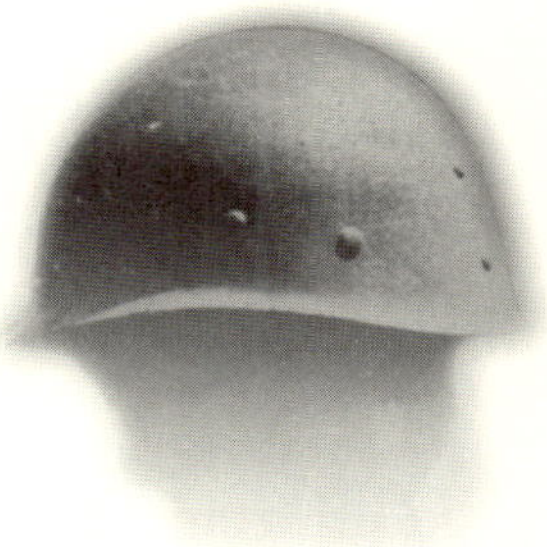

Chapter Seven

Battlefield Bound

It is impossible to know what was going through the minds of the men on September 4, 1944, as they were loading onto the ship to depart from the safety of the Boston port and aware that they were headed for the battlefield of France. These men had already endured basic training and then months of battlefield training at various sites in the United States (the 44th actually started their training at Fort Lewis, Washington, before Dad joined the 324th Regiment in Louisiana). Dad had gone through the disappointment of not finishing his college education and, along with other former ASTP students, had the accelerated education in that program abruptly terminated. Even with these challenges already met, the soldiers of the 44th probably had no idea of the mental stress, emotional anxiety, and physical hardship that was before them.

There was no way for any of us to really know what these men went through and the sacrifice they made. We can only remember that they *did* sacrifice, and we can have an appreciation for the extent of that sacrifice by recalling specific events that they and others have chronicled for us. Dad's letters while in the battlefield are a part of that chronicle.

All soldiers had to limit what they could reveal in letters and cards sent home. While he was in combat, nearly all of the letters that Dad wrote were stamped and signed by an Army examiner to verify that the content was OK (a couple letters must have slipped through because there was no noticeable examiner stamp on the face of the letter). In one letter (October 22, 1944) it appears as though five words were censored by the examiner. Not even a hint of specific locations, experiences of battle, or information about plans could be mentioned in these letters home.

Consequently, to give a more complete picture of Dad's combat experiences, I have utilized information from the *Combat History of the 324th Infantry Regiment* and the website of the 44th Division.[3,4] These sources provide a specific timeline for the 324th Regiment, specific dates of battles with locations, description of the terrain, weather and other battlefield conditions, and in some cases, the morale of the men. Dad's experiences would have been the same as those described in these sources, particularly the *Combat History of the 324th Infantry Regiment* since generally the entire regiment advanced toward the same goal in a coordinated fashion. At times these sources specifically mention Company C of the First Battalion in terms of their location or battlefield objective.

V-MAIL

With the exception of the last letter that Dad wrote on the battlefield, all of his letters written on the battlefield to my grandparents were V-mail (Victory Mail). V-mail was a means to greatly reduce the size and weight of the tons of letters coming from and going to the battlefield. The letter was written on specific V-mail stationary that was 7 x $9\frac{1}{8}$ inches and contained a glued flap that was folded to create its own envelope. The letter sent by an overseas soldier was opened by military personnel at a receiving station overseas, censored by the military examiners, and then photographed onto reels of microfilm. The film was transported by airplane to the United States and then a reduced-sized facsimile was printed from the film. The printed version was $4\frac{1}{4}$ x $5\frac{3}{16}$ inches (about postcard size). The top portion contained the address and was pre-creased so when folded, it would fit into a window-style envelope with the address showing.

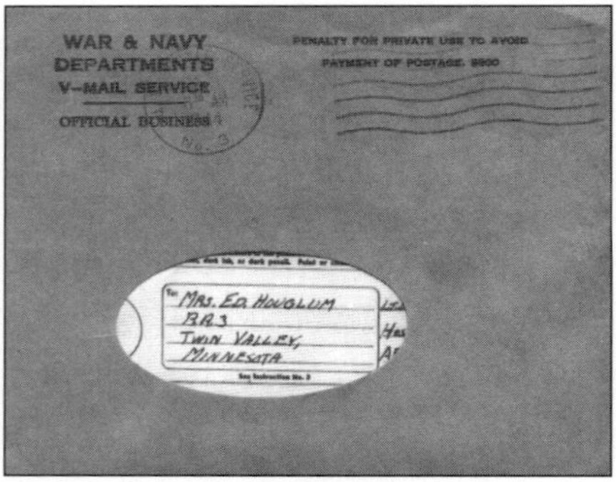

The envelope for V-mail delivery.

According to the Postal Museum website,[6] it would take thirty-seven mail bags to hold 150,000 one-page letters but would only take one mail bag to hold the film for the same number of V-mail letters, reducing the weight from 2,575 pounds to 45 pounds. This space and weight conserved on transport planes could then be used for supplies and equipment. Between June 15, 1942, and April 1, 1945, over 556 million pieces of V-mail were sent to service men from the United States

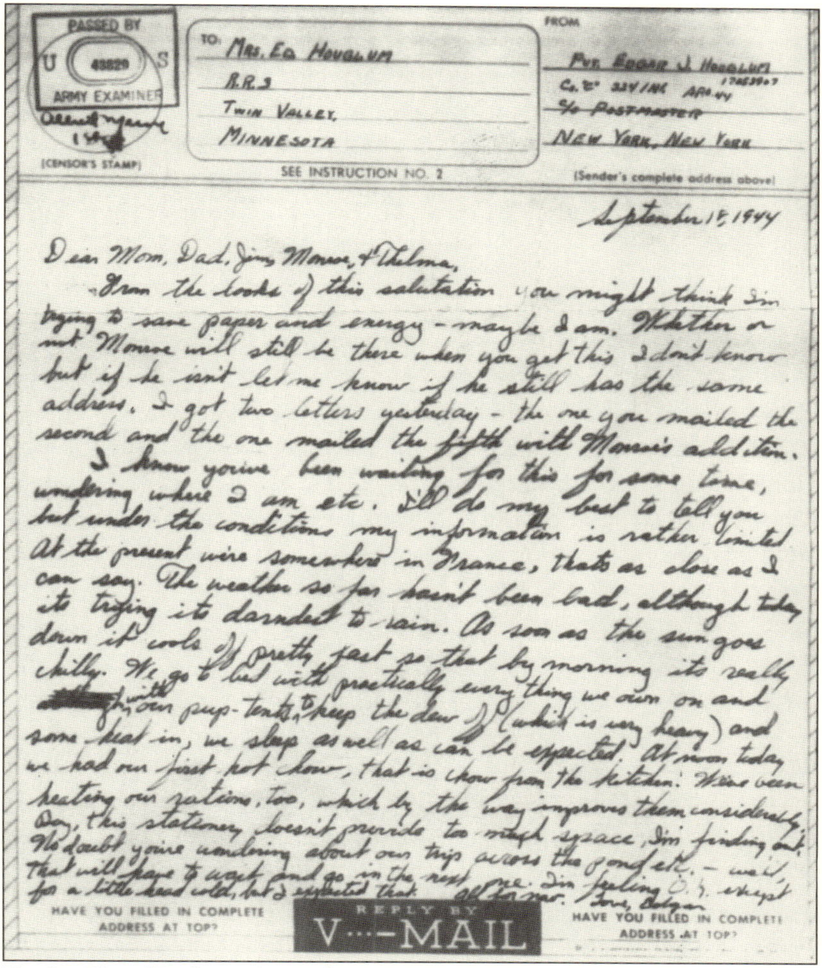
PASSED BY
U.S.
ARMY EXAMINER
(CENSOR'S STAMP)

TO: MRS. ED HOVGLUM
R.R. 3
TWIN VALLEY,
MINNESOTA

SEE INSTRUCTION NO. 2

FROM
PVT. EDGAR J. HOVGLUM
Co. "E" 334/INF APO #
c/o POSTMASTER
NEW YORK, NEW YORK
(Sender's complete address above)

September 18, 1944

Dear Mom, Dad, Jim, Monroe, & Thelma,

From the looks of this salutation you might think I'm trying to save paper and energy — maybe I am. Whether or not Monroe will still be there when you get this I don't know but if he isn't let me know if he still has the same address. I got two letters yesterday — the one you mailed the second and the one mailed the fifth with Monroe's addition.

I know you've been waiting for this for some time, wondering where I am etc. I'll do my best to tell you but under the conditions my information is rather limited. At the present we're somewhere in France, that's as close as I can say. The weather so far hasn't been bad, although today it's trying its darndest to rain. As soon as the sun goes down it cools off pretty fast so that by morning it's really chilly. We go to bed with practically everything we own on and [redacted] with our pup-tents to keep the dew off (which is very heavy) and some heat in, we sleep as well as can be expected. At noon today we had our first hot chow, that is chow from the kitchen. We've been heating our rations, too, which by the way improves them considerably. Boy, this stationery doesn't provide too much space, I'm finding out. No doubt you're wondering about our trip across the pond etc. — well, that will have to wait and so in the next one. I'm feeling O.K. except for a little head cold, but I expected that. All for now. Love, Edgar

HAVE YOU FILLED IN COMPLETE ADDRESS AT TOP?

REPLY BY V···–MAIL

HAVE YOU FILLED IN COMPLETE ADDRESS AT TOP?

The first V-mail Dad sent, September 18, 1944.

and over 510 million pieces were sent by military personnel overseas to the United States; of this total, Dad's contribution in pieces sent to his parents was twenty-seven.

One disadvantage of V-mail was that the print was reduced to sixty percent of the original size, making the V-mail difficult to read, especially if the writer had small handwriting to begin with. Even though Dad had good penmanship, a magnifying glass was the only way to identify some words in some of his V-mails. Just as on a postcard when the writer starts running out of space, the hand writing often got smaller as Dad approached the bottom of the page.

All of Dad's 27 V-mails were addressed to "Mrs. Ed Houglum, R.R. 3, Twin Valley, Minnesota, except two which were sent specifically to my grandfather for his birthday. The salutation was always "Dear Mom, Dad, & Jim," on each V-mail except for the two to my grandfather and one other which included "Monroe, & Thelma" in the salutation. Without exception, he ended each letter, "Love, Edgar."

France and More Training

The 44th Division left Boston on September 5, 1944, aboard the *U.S.S. William H. Gordon,* landing in Cherbourg, France, on September 15th. Dad didn't write any letters while in route across the Atlantic, but he wrote two V-mails on September 18th. He was sea-sick for a couple days which reminded him of the stomach flu. He also wrote that he could not be specific as to his whereabouts *"we're somewhere in France, that's as close as I can say."*

> *... I know you've been waiting for this for some time, wondering where I am etc. I'll do my best to tell you but under the conditions my information is rather limited. At the present we're somewhere in France, that's as close as I can say. The weather so far hasn't been bad, although today its trying its darndest to rain. As soon as the sun goes down it cools off pretty fast so that by morning its really chilly. We go to bed with practically every thing we own on and with our pup-tents to keep the dew off (which is very heavy) and some heat in, we sleep as well as can be expected. At noon today we had our first hot chow, that*

is chow from the kitchen. We've been heating our rations, too, which by the way improves them considerably. Boy, this stationary doesn't provide too much space, I'm finding out. No doubt you're wondering about our trip across the pond etc. – well, that will have to wait and go in the next one. I'm feeling O.K. except for a little head cold, but I expected that. All for now.

Love,
Edgar

Dear Mom, Dad, & Jim,

I just wrote you a letter a little while ago, but one sheet of this abbreviated stationary wasn't quite big enough.

I re-read one of your letters and noticed that I was aboard ship the day Monroe got home. We had walked up the gang plank the day before we were some of the first ones loaded and so had to spend a little over a day on the ship before we sailed. Quarters on the ship were crowded, our bunks were arranged four high with just enough room to crawl in and out. I was one of the many men on detail on the way across and so had three meals a day – everyone else had just two, morning and afternoon. I worked from midnight until 8 o'clock but several nights the crew on duty before us had everything taken care of so we got off early. The first few days out were not very enjoyable for lots of the boys including me. The second day I began feeling dizzy and woozy – what I ate started coming up again but it hadn't tasted very good anyway so it didn't matter. We were told to keep eating so we would have something to heave up and that a full stomach would help. Towards evening of our third day I started feeling better and from then on I was O.K. It reminded me of the times I had stomach flu – remember? To begin with you feel like you've had a few drinks too many – everything turns one way or another. Guess I'll have to save what I have left for the next letter.

Love,
Edgar

Cherbourg, the landing site for the 324th, is located along the English Channel in northern France, in the region referred to as Normandy. The 324th spent about a month in Normandy for their final combat preparations. During that month, Dad wrote six V-mail letters home. Two V-mail on September 18th regarding his trip across the Atlantic and landing in France, and then letters about a week apart for the next three weeks with two on October 1st.

On Monday, September 25th, Dad wrote a letter regarding his weekend activities. He said that the previous Saturday afternoon he had time off and did his laundry. On Sunday he *"shaved and cleaned up a bit… "* and then when to church, *"Well, my first church service on foreign soil turned out to be a communion service too, so I guess its one I'll remember."* It was nice to read that they had some relaxation time as Dad wrote that in the afternoon his platoon played other platoons in games of softball and his platoon won all three games by scores of 7-6, 7-6, and 10-3. In one of his October 1st letters he also said that they had another softball game on Saturday, September 30th, and his team won 13-4 and that he was the first baseman for his platoon. During all of the years that I played baseball from grade school through high school, first base was my primary position. I wonder if Dad thought of these games in France while watching me play his position. Dad finished his weekend activities with an old movie and ends the letter on the 25th by saying,

> *As much as I hate to admit it, our chow seems to be slipping. What we get is good, but not enough to suit most every one. As yet we haven't seen any thing of a P.X. either, so if you decide to send any thing, sweets would taste pretty good – chocolate drops, cookies etc. You might include a good wrist watch straps in that too. Goodnight for now.*
>
> *Love,*
> *Edgar*

Interestingly, the letter of September 25th must have taken about a month to reach home because the letter has a Twin Valley postmark of October 23rd. In his first letter of October 1st, he mentioned that he received that day their letter postmarked the 7th even though a few days previously he had received the one postmarked the 9th. He hoped that his mail wasn't taking that long to get home but that *"all the fellows are having the same trouble."*

It seems odd, but military personnel were often paid in local currency; the theory being the soldiers could spend it if they wanted. Dad wrote on October 1st, *"Yesterday we got payed – all in francs. By the looks of my billfold, I'll be sending some of it as soon as I can."* He mentioned it again a month later in his letter of November 2nd, *"Well, yesterday we got paid and as I haven't spent a cent (or a franc) for some time I'm sending what I have this time home - $10 to be exact. I've still got almost $15 left from before."* Some of the francs he never spent and are still among his military effects.

A common theme throughout many of the letters was the weather. Not only from Dad, but also to Dad from home. In these letters from Normandy, the soldiers were already enduring what they would experience all too frequently during the coming months, rain and mud.

> *It seems that what you might call the rainy season has set in here. Hardly a day goes by that we don't have some showers. As yet, though there haven't been any heavy rains, usually a cold drizzle.* (October 1)

> *Today the weather went back to normal again – more rain, and its still cloudy so we can probably expect the same tomorrow. In places around here its beginning to get a bit on the muddy side, especially along the main thorough fares in the area.* (October 9)

> *We're still walking in mud, and although it hasn't rained quite as much for the past couple of days the moisture doesn't disappear – the ground is too well saturated.* (October 22)

The invasion of Normandy by the Allies had occurred on D-Day, June 6, 1944. The landing beaches of Normandy, such as Utah and Omaha beaches, were within a few miles of where the 324th was training. In a letter of October 22nd, Dad's regiment had already been trans-

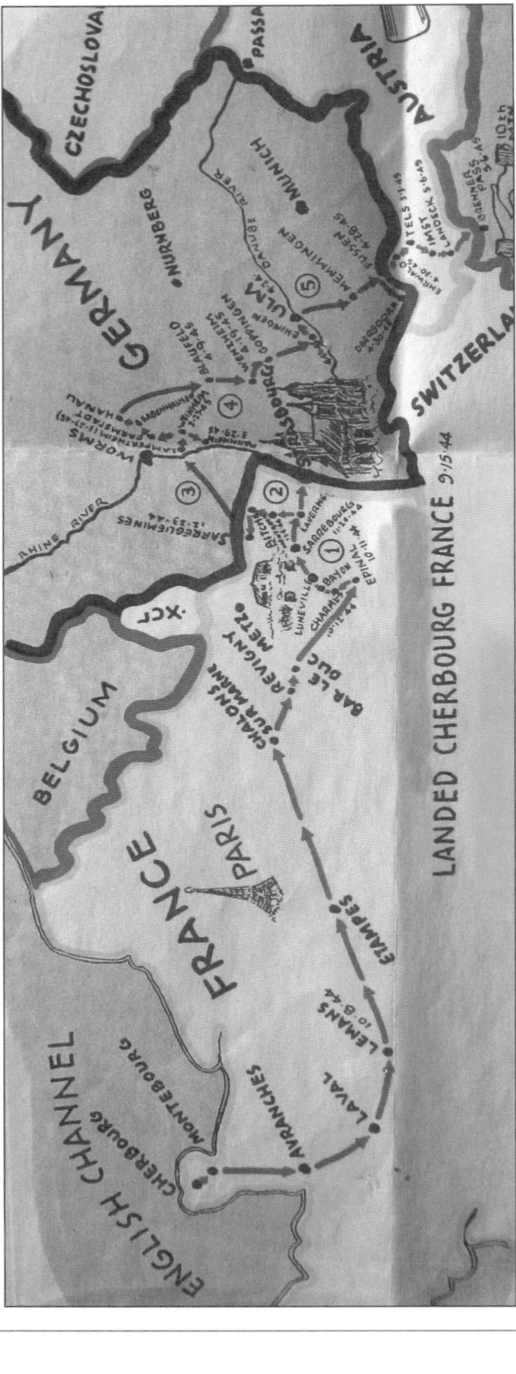

An overview of the route traveled by 324th Regiment during World War II. (Taken from 44th Infantry Highlights Map)

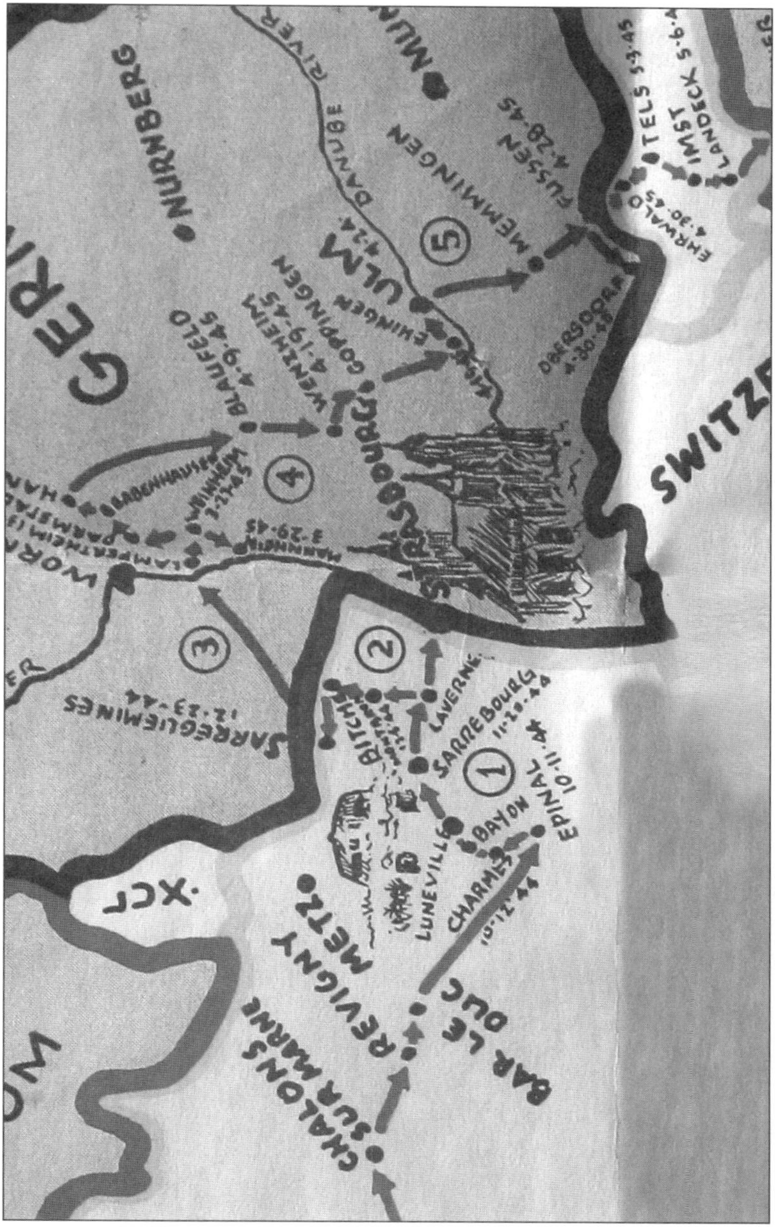

A close-up look of the route traveled by 324th Regiment during World War II. (Taken from 44th Infantry Highlights Map)

ported to the combat zone and the next day would be the first death from their regiment. He hadn't written for a couple weeks, but since he couldn't say much of his current situation he mentioned visiting the beaches of Normandy.

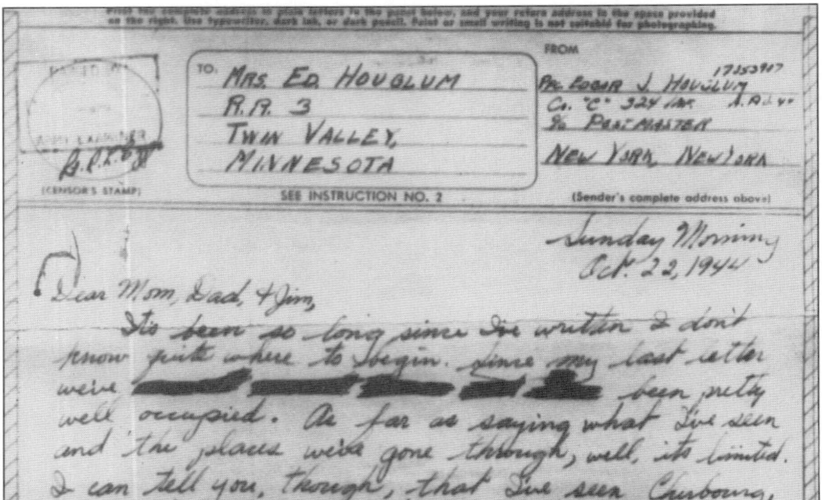

TO: MRS. ED HOUGLUM
R.R. 3
TWIN VALLEY,
MINNESOTA

FROM
17153917
Pvt. Edgar J. Houglum
Co. "C" 324 Inf. A.P.O.
% Postmaster
New York, New York

(CENSOR'S STAMP)
SEE INSTRUCTION NO. 2
(Sender's complete address above)

Sunday Morning
Oct. 22, 1944

Dear Mom, Dad, & Jim,

It's been so long since I've written I don't know quite where to begin. Since my last letter we've [redacted] been pretty well occupied. As far as saying what I've seen and the places we've gone through, well, it's limited. I can tell you, though, that I've seen Cherbourg, and while we were at our first bivouac area we visited the beach where the invasion took place. France has a lot of beautiful scenery, and under other conditions I believe a person might even enjoy seeing it.

We're still walking in mud, and although it hasn't rained quite as much for the past couple of days the moisture doesn't disappear – the ground is too well saturated.

I don't know when I'll be able to write or get any mail again, but don't worry – as I said before, no news is good news. I got a letter from you last Thursday – the last mail call we had. That's all for this time – I'll write as soon as I can.

Love, Edgar

HAVE YOU FILLED IN COMPLETE ADDRESS AT TOP?

V-MAIL

HAVE YOU FILLED IN COMPLETE ADDRESS AT TOP?

A V-mail written on October 22, 1944.

Dear Mom, Dad, & Jim,

It's been so long since I've written I don't know quite where to begin. Since my last letter we've been pretty well occupied. As far as saying what I've seen and the places we've gone through, well, its limited. I can tell you, though, that I've seen Cherbourg, and while we were at our fist bivouac area we visited the beach where the invasion took place. France has a lot of beautiful scenery, and under other conditions I believe a person might even enjoy seeing it.

We're still walking in mud, and although it hasn't rained quite as much for the past couple of days the moisture doesn't disappear – the ground is too well saturated.

I don't know when I'll be able to write or get any mail off again, but don't worry – as I said before, no news is good news. I got a letter from you last Thursday – the last mail call we had. That's all for this time- I'll write as soon as I can.

Love,
Edgar

The invasion of Normandy was a key to the success of the Allies in Europe because it gave them a secure foothold and eventually allowed them to push the enemy out of France and back into Germany. The operation was massive; in fact, one of the code names was Overload. On D-Day approximately 140,000 troops landed, 6,939 naval vessels were involved and 12,000 aircraft. By June 12th, over 300,000 troops had landed; by June 19th the number of U.S. and British troops was over 300,000 each, and by July 4th, the total number of Allied troops had grown to over one million.[7] By the end of August the port at Cherbourg had been captured, which allowed the landing of the 44th Division; now it was their turn to push the German army back farther.

I'm guessing that in the face of impending danger, it is common for people to become more reflective. At this point Dad's regiment was making their last preparations for battle; the men did not know exactly where they were headed, except going into battle was imminent. Dad's opening sentence in his letter of October 1st is, *"Another week beginning and also the start of a new month – can't help but wonder what it has to offer."* On October 9th, after evidently receiving a letter from home regarding a friend getting married, Dad wrote, *"So the people back there are still getting married... Seems to me that most of them are just "kids" yet. Maybe I am getting older than I realize."* Dad was twenty-two years old.

The Front Lines

On October 13th, the 44th Division began moving out of Normandy to a town called Luneville in eastern France. Some of the men were transported by rail, others by trucks. It was a long trip, about 400 miles as the crow flies, and took until the17th for everyone to arrive. Virtually all of the combat in France for the 324th occurred in the Alsace-Lorraine region. These provinces are along the German border. The Vosges Mountains are the most notable geographic obstacle that spreads across much of Alsace, running north and south.

The mission for the 44th Division was to replace the 79th Division on line. Each battalion of the 324th Regiment was designated a specific position for a replacement of specific infantry regiments of the 79th Division. On October 24th, the 324th relieved the men who had been on the front lines. German artillery and tanks caused some casualties during this process. At this point, the 324th Infantry had about 2,250 front line combat troops. The German army directly in front had about 1,050 men with another 4,500 in immediate reserve. Within a few hours of replacing their comrades, the 324th Regiment lost its commander when he was killed by a land mine.[3]

The first day on line, as well as the remaining days of October, quickly initiated the 324th into combat with enemy artillery and air attacks and through patrols that were sent out. According to the *Combat History of the 324th,* the excellent work of these patrols as they clashed with the enemy and reported reconnaissance information earned commendations but also casualties. The *Combat History,* page 74, describes the experience of patrol duty as, *"that feeling of utter isolation and a tension unequaled in almost any other form of combat activity."* I remember Dad telling the story of being on a patrol early in his battlefield experience, being cut off from their unit for a period of time while the patrol was under fire, and losing a significant portion of the men in his patrol. Whether Dad earned a commendation during this specific event or not, is unknown, but Dad earned a Bronze Star during this time frame. The citation reads:

> By direction of the President, under the provisions of Executive Order 9419, 4 February 1944 (Sec. II, WD Bul. 43, 1944), you have been awarded the Bronze Star Medal for exemplary conduct in ground combat against the armed enemy while assigned as Private First Class, 324th Infantry Regiment, on or about 29 October 1944, in the European Theater of Operations.

Many brave acts of heroism by members of the 324th were displayed within the first week of combat, which resulted in awards of a Distinguished Service Cross, two Silver Stars, Combat Infantrymen's Badges, and Purple Hearts. Unfortunately, casualties come with heroism; sixty-eight reinforcements joined them on October 27th and 28th to replace the casualties already incurred.

It is amazing to me that the Germans and the Americans each knew much of what the other was doing relative to troop movements. For example, the Germans beamed propaganda toward the Americans saying, *"Hello men of the 44th. Thanks for relieving the men of the 79th Division. This is going to be a bloody mess... Come over with your hands raised..."* (*Combat History of 324th,* page 19).

During the last few days of October, Dad's regiment reinforced their defensive positions (foxholes), warded off enemy combat patrols, and sent out their own patrols as part of the preparation for forward movement and attack. The foxholes were home for these men during this time. They used tree branches and whatever they could find to protect themselves from rain and to keep some heat inside the foxhole. The wet weather and mud were problematic, and thus a system was set up for the regiment to launder clothes at points removed from the front lines and then redistribute them to the men. Companies rotated off the front line for a change of clothes, hot meals, a shower, and to write a letter (see excerpt from Dad's letter of November 10th on pages 67).

The rain, cold, and mud were disheartening and added to the monotony as days passed with the men trying to stay dry and warm, as well as safe from shells and shrapnel. When it was safe from enemy fire, they had to dump water out of their foxholes or moved around just to keep

Foxholes were home for days and sometimes weeks at a time. (Taken from *Combat History of 44th Infantry Division*)[8]

warm. The monotony must have been bad because some men volunteered for reconnaissance patrols, although sometimes they didn't all make it back. It was in this setting that Dad wrote a couple of letters. He mentioned that he hadn't written for awhile but that,

> *... there seems to be less and less to write about. I've been standing here long enough to write several of these trying to find something to put down. About all I can think of is that I'm still O.K. and that we're doing the best we can under the circumstances – I can say its not much of an atmosphere for writing letters.* (October 30, 1944)

On November 2nd, Dad began to write another letter but again he was not sure what to write, *"so I'll talk first about the weather."* He mentioned the rain and mud. Then he lets his family know for certain what they probably already suspected, *"If you haven't already guessed it, I can now tell you that I'm on the front lines."* Even if my grandparents suspected as much, I'm sure it literally brought home the realization that their son was in harm's way daily.

I cannot adequately realize what my grandparents must have felt, but having had a daughter in a war zone when Operation Iraqi Freedom began on March 20, 2003, I think I can empathize somewhat. For me, the two most stressful occasions during the months that our daughter was a part of this Gulf War were the night she called us to say "goodbye" as her company was leaving Fort Sill for the Gulf and preparation for conflict, and then the night I heard the war had actually begun, which was followed by three weeks without any communication from her. I'll never forget the emotions of those occasions.

Considering the large-scale nature of World War II, that the war had already been ongoing for years, and that there had already been thousands of casualties, the stress and anxiety experienced by parents, wives, and other family members must have been intense. But yet these family members went on with their daily lives; it helped to take their minds off the thought of receiving a notification from the War Department that they never wanted to see. When we appreciate the sacrifices made during World War II, the family members of that generation should not be forgotten either.

Promotions

According to the *Combat History of the 324th,* patrols were sent out more frequently during the first few days of November. Even though roads and fields were muddy and soaked, patrols were sent *"sloshing away into enemy territory."* In a letter Dad wrote on November 5th, he lets my grandparents know that he was sending home to them a good conduct ribbon for one year of duty, and,

> *... a "combat infantryman's badge." Quite a few men in the company received them yesterday for a certain bit of action we went through. By the way, it is exactly the same as the expert infantryman's badge I got back there except that this one has the wreath added.*

Evidently my grandparents hadn't seen that after September 18th Dad had changed his rank in the return address on the V-mail from "PVT" (private) to "PFC" (private first class) and they must have apologized for the oversight in a letter they sent. Of course, true to his nature, Dad did not specifically mention the promotion in any of his V-mails. The promotion, and my grandparents' concern for their oversight, was one topic in his letter of November 10th; he also wrote about shaving, the letters he has received from home, and the impact of the weather on their foxholes.

Dear Mom, Dad, & Jim,

I just finished chopping off about a week's beard and even though my hands are cold and a little hard to manipulate I thought I'd better write while they're at least clean.

I've had several letters from you now since the last time I wrote, the last one was dated the 23rd. As far as your not seeing that little promotion of some time ago, you don't have to worry about it. As a matter of fact I can't say I had been noticing how my mail was addressed. You couldn't have missed very many anyway because I think I got it about the middle of September.

Weather conditions here are still a long ways from being pleasant. The last week almost its been raining just about all the time. Yesterday we even had a little snow mixed with it. Our [fox] *holes give us the most trouble as its hard to keep the water from soaking through on all sides as well as coming through the opening. Guess I'll have to write another one of these.*

Love,
Edgar

Dad wrote a second letter on November 10th since he didn't have enough room on just one V-mail. Again the weather entered into the letter but for a different reason.

Dear Mom, Dad, & Jim,

Here comes the second part of this so called letter. I wasn't quite through when I reached the bottom of the other one. I hope they both get there the same day or things might sound a little confused.

Some time ago we were issued a new type of shoe or boot to help keep our feet dry. They have rubber bottoms and leather tops similar to those shoe-pacs you've seen. They are a big help too but even with them its about impossible to stay dry all the time. Boy, I've never slopped around in so much mud in all my life and I hope its soon over.

One day last week we were taken into a town back a little ways for what was to us a real treat. We were given a good hot shower, a hot meal, and all clean clothes and blankets. The only thing, the stuff didn't have a chance to stay clean very long in these conditions.

324th Infantry Regiment, First Battalion on the move. (Taken from *Combat History of the 324th Infantry Regiment*)[3]

Well, I think I'm about through now so I'll have to call it quits. Must have been quite a birthday party you had. Don't forget to get yourself something for me. 'Bye for now.

Love,
Edgar

Dad received another promotion on November 7th, to corporal, to sergeant later in the month, and then to staff sergeant on December 18th. His return address reflected these changes, but the content of his letters did not. Whether my grandparents commented in other letters about these promotions is uncertain since we have no letters from my grandparents to Dad during the time he was in Europe. After Dad's first promotion, they most likely were more cognizant of Dad's rank on the return address of his V-mails.

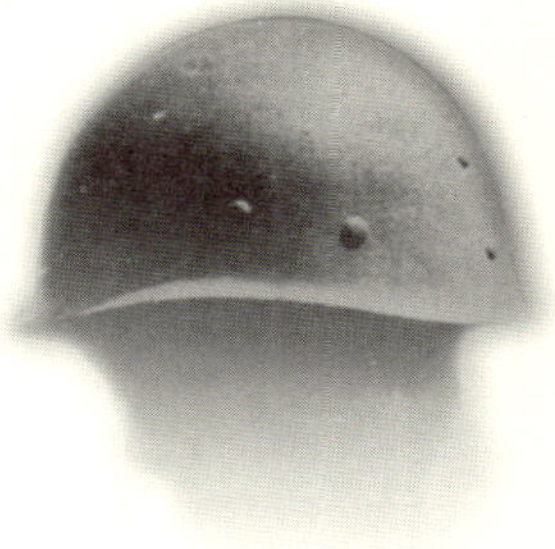

Chapter Eight

Pushing Toward The German Border

By mid-November 1944, the battles of the 324th had been in France and the Regiment was in Embermenil. Of course, the objective was to push the German army completely out of France and back into Germany. Sarrebourg is less than forty miles from the German border and Strasbourg is at the border where the Rhine River separates the two countries; the Vosges Mountains are in between. Because the intent of this document is to give the reader a general idea of the events that Dad and his comrades experienced, provided here is a brief summary of some events leading to the liberation of Sarrebourg, the continued push toward Strasbourg, and the re-direction north as December came to a close.

Sarrebourg Objective

The reconnaissance patrols were part of the preparation for an attack on the enemy with the goal to push them back to Sarrebourg, about twenty miles closer to the German border. The attack began on November 13th. Dad's next V-mail was November 30th, and this summary provides a backdrop for that letter. The *Combat History of the 324th*[3] provides a detailed account of the Regiment's experiences for the remaining days of November; that document is the primary source of the summary of information provided here regarding this push toward Germany.

After a barrage of artillery fire throughout the night from both sides, the attack by the 324th was set to begin at exactly 0700. Men waited in their foxholes, counting the minutes and seconds before they moved out of their foxholes and into their uncertain destiny. Each battalion and company had their orders and knew the plan. There was deep snow on the ground and fog in the air. Machine gun and sniper fire, as well as poor visibility, hampered progress early in the battle. One company suffered thirty casualties in fifteen minutes as bodies lie in the snow in an open field between the Americans and Germans. The German vantage point on higher ground was such that some wounded men lay in the cold and snow for a long time before anyone could get to them. Company C of the First Battalion was among the groups of men who had to fall back temporarily because of the fierce enemy fire. Heavy fighting continued for a few days as the Americans slowly pushed forward.

The three battalions of the 324th fought over rough terrain, through cold and snow, and suffered heavy casualties. Heroic efforts by many individuals to assist wounded men and to knock out key machine gun sites, plus maneuvers by other division forces, enabled the Regiment to finally come close to the strategically significant town of Avricourt.

To reach the outskirts of the town had already cost many American casualties. The First and Second Battalions had approached the town at night and as they dug in their foxholes they realized that they had gone beyond some German outposts and were too close to the German main line of resistance. Consequently the German forces bombarded the battalions with mortar shells. During the night, the First and Second Battalions prevented the attempts by the Germans to surround them.

In the meantime, elements of the Third Battalion had approached Avricourt from another direction. They were also dug into foxholes, waiting for reinforcements before they would try to take the city in daylight; but there were no reinforcements. They waited for orders the next morning, hoping in vain they would see fresh troops to assist. The Regiment had come through days of heavy fighting and the men were tired and cold.

The *Combat History of the 324th,* page 32, gives an account of one company that had suffered heavy losses, was fatigued from hard fighting in bitter weather, and had some men limping from trench foot. The response of these men when they heard the orders to attack Avricourt even though there were no reinforcements was, "[they] *were very quiet and some of them wept unashamed.*" They had to do it... so they did. These men left their foxholes because they were the only forces that were within striking distance of the city. Of this same company, the account says, *"Most of the men didn't care what happened to them anymore."*

If the Germans would have known the mental and physical condition of these American troops, maybe their strategy would have been different. When the Americans entered the town, to their surprise and joy, the German troops rose from their trenches and hiding places with their hands raised in surrender. As the rest of the 324th entered the town, with the aid of a tank battalion, they also saw the enemy surrendering or running away.

There were many other small towns in route to Sarrebourg that the 324th needed to take from the Germans, but none was more difficult as the route to Avricourt. The next day the Regiment continued to push forward and took Deutsch-Avricourt after one hour of fighting, and then Rechicourt. The Germans continued to surrender in large numbers as other towns were captured, Bois de Ketzing, Haut-Clocher, and Langate.

On November 21st, the 324th was given a rest and a letter of commendation was issued to the 44th Division by General Patch, Commanding General of the Seventh Army.

After one day of rest, the 324th moved at a rapid rate and continued beyond Sarrebourg to take the towns of Hangviller, Schoenbourg, Bust, Dossenheim, Neuwiller, Griesbach, and Hattmat. The Regiment had now gone through the pass of the Vosges Mountains that ran through the region of Alsace and along the eastern edge of France and were further east than any other unit of the Seventh Army. Strasbourg was at the border on the Rhine River that separated France and Germany and was only a few miles away and had been liberated by other elements of the Seventh Army. Strasbourg was originally selected as the key entry point into Germany but maneuvers by the German army and reconsideration by General Eisenhower changed the plans for the Americans. The new orders were to move north for an alternate point of crossing into Germany.

On November 28th, the 324th Regiment was relieved by the entire 100th Division. Once relieved, they traveled back through the Vosges Mountains and into an area that had already been secured. On the 28th they were in a town called Rauwiller, and on the 29th they moved to

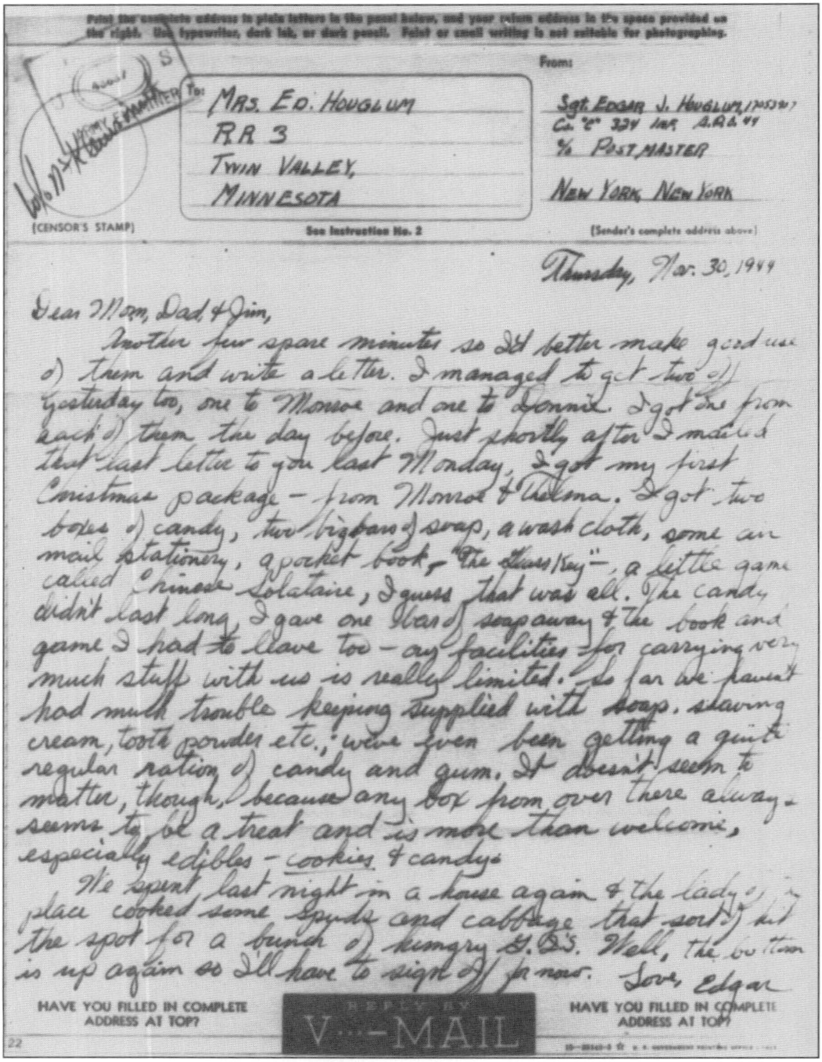

Print the complete address in plain letters in the panel below, and your return address in the space provided on the right. Use typewriter, dark ink, or dark pencil. Faint or small writing is not suitable for photographing.

To: MRS. ED. HOUGLUM
RR 3
TWIN VALLEY,
MINNESOTA

From: Sgt. Edgar J. Houglum
Co. "E" 324 Inf. A.P.O. 44
% Post Master
New York, New York

(CENSOR'S STAMP) See Instruction No. 2 (Sender's complete address above)

Thursday, Nov. 30, 1944

Dear Mom, Dad & Jim,

Another few spare minutes so I'd better make good use of them and write a letter. I managed to get two off yesterday too, one to Monroe and one to Donnie. I got one from each of them the day before. Just shortly after I mailed that last letter to you last Monday, I got my first Christmas package — from Monroe & Thelma. I got two boxes of candy, two big bars of soap, a wash cloth, some air mail stationery, a pocket book, "The Glass Key" — a little game called Chinese Solataire, I guess that was all. The candy didn't last long, I gave one bar of soap away & the book and game I had to leave too — our facilities for carrying very much stuff with us is really limited. So far we haven't had much trouble keeping supplied with soap, shaving cream, tooth powder etc.; we've even been getting a quite regular ration of candy and gum. It doesn't seem to matter, though, because any box from over there always seems to be a treat and is more than welcome, especially edibles — cookies & candys.

We spent last night in a house again & the lady of the place cooked some spuds and cabbage that sort of hit the spot for a bunch of hungry G.I.'s. Well, the bottom is up again so I'll have to sign off for now. Love, Edgar

HAVE YOU FILLED IN COMPLETE ADDRESS AT TOP? REPLY BY V-MAIL HAVE YOU FILLED IN COMPLETE ADDRESS AT TOP?

A V-mail written November 30, 1944.

Siewiller. Based on Dad's letter of November 30th, evidently the soldiers had the simple luxury of getting out of the cold weather as they spent the night in the houses of those towns. In that letter home Dad described his previous night, *"We spent last night in a house again & the lady of the place cooked some spuds and cabbage that sort of hit the spot for a bunch of hungry G.I.'s."* I'm sure the French woman of the house was glad to hear English spoken in the house rather than German. Dad also mentions in this letter that he received his first Christmas package which was from Monroe and Thelma.

> *I got two boxes of candy, two big bars of soap, a wash cloth, some air mail stationery, a pocket book – "The Glass Key" – a little game called Chinese Solataire, I guess that was all. The candy didn't last long, I gave one bar of soap away & the book and game I had to leave too – our facilities for carrying very much stuff with us is really limited. So far we haven't had much trouble keeping supplied with soap, shaving cream, tooth powder etc.; we've even been getting a quite regular ration of candy and gum. It doesn't seem to matter, though, because any box from over there always seems to be a treat and is more than welcome, especially edibles – cookies & candy.*

Christmas 1944

To begin December the troops of the 324th were rested; as it turned out, they were to need it. The Regiment moved north against heavy enemy resistance to take Waldhambach on December 2nd, and then continued north and met an enemy force that was dug in. As in other battles that are described in detail in the *Combat History of the 324th,* heroic efforts by individual soldiers were key to the victory of individual battles, battle after battle. Men took the lead to take out enemy tanks, machine guns, or other elements that were hindering the success of their mission. In some cases these heroes paid the ultimate sacrifice as they successfully eliminated their target. In the battles of early December, each company saw the brave actions of their buddies. Heavy fighting for three days in the area of Ratzwiller took heavy casualties as ground was slowly taken, lost, and regained.

After Ratzwiller, the Regiment continued on December 5th to move north more rapidly, with the objective being Petit-Rederching several miles away. The terrain included forest and open areas. The Germans had substantial forces in this area. After a few days of reconnaissance and regrouping, the 324th initiated an attack led by the First Battalion. During the attack, elements of A, C, and D companies were separated from the rest of their companies for several hours. On December 12th, B and C companies reached Petit-Rederching, but not without heroic efforts, as well as casualties, including the First Battalion commander.

The Regiment saw continued heavy fighting as it moved north of Petit-Rederching. As they advanced to the Schwalb River, enemy fire prevented the engineers from constructing a suitable bridge for crossing. Through diversion tactics and flanking maneuvers, the enemy was removed from the area sufficiently for the bridge to be built. After fifteen days of intense combat, the 324th was relieved by the 124th Regiment and allowed to rest at Lembach, located about twenty miles to the east.

One of two Christmas cards Dad obtained that was provided by the Army. This one he sent to Monroe and Thelma on December 15, 1944. The other he sent home.

On December 21st, the Regiment was transported about thirty miles northwest, just east of Sarreguemines, to the towns of Bliesbruck and Frauenberg. They relieve the 35th Division, which had obtained a location beyond the Blies River which separates a small portion of France and Germany in northeastern France. Attacks by the enemy resulted in men being killed and captured, and eventually the order to withdraw back across the Blies during the night of December 23rd. This was the only withdrawal from its combat position for the 324th Regiment during World War II. It was with these recent events that Dad spent Christmas 1944, a couple miles from the German border. His letter of Christmas reflects some melancholy, no doubt from not only the recent withdrawal of the Regiment, but also the fierce fighting he had experienced for more than two months.

Monday
December 25, 1944

Dear Mom, Dad, & Jim,

Merry Christmas to you all!

Christmas Day, 1944 – a day I'm quite sure I won't forget and hope it's the last one there is with the world in the condition it is.

I'm afraid I picked a poor time to write – not in the mood I guess but I should be able to fill a page like this.

I'm sitting in a barn door with the sun coming in sixty per. It is a beautiful December day here, as far as weather conditions go, clear as a bell but a little crisp and chilly. In fact the last few days haven't been too bad, cold alright but dry at least. The nights really get you chilled clear through too.

I don't know why it is, but there is something about a day like today that makes a fellow think a lot more than usual – at any rate I've been doing quite a bit [of] *both last night and today.*

There was a rumor around last night that we were supposed to have turkey for chow but it was frozen so hard they couldn't get it thawed out in time – probably get it today.

Well, that's about all for this time again. I'm already thinking about the New Year, hoping it'll see better conditions for everyone.

Love,
Edgar

The last several days of December were used by the Regiment to regroup, conduct reconnaissance, and improve their current position. It gave Dad time to catch up on his letter writing and talk about the Christmas dinner that he was anticipating when he was writing his previous letter. Even though he was in the midst of the battle zone, he evidently had received Christmas packages.

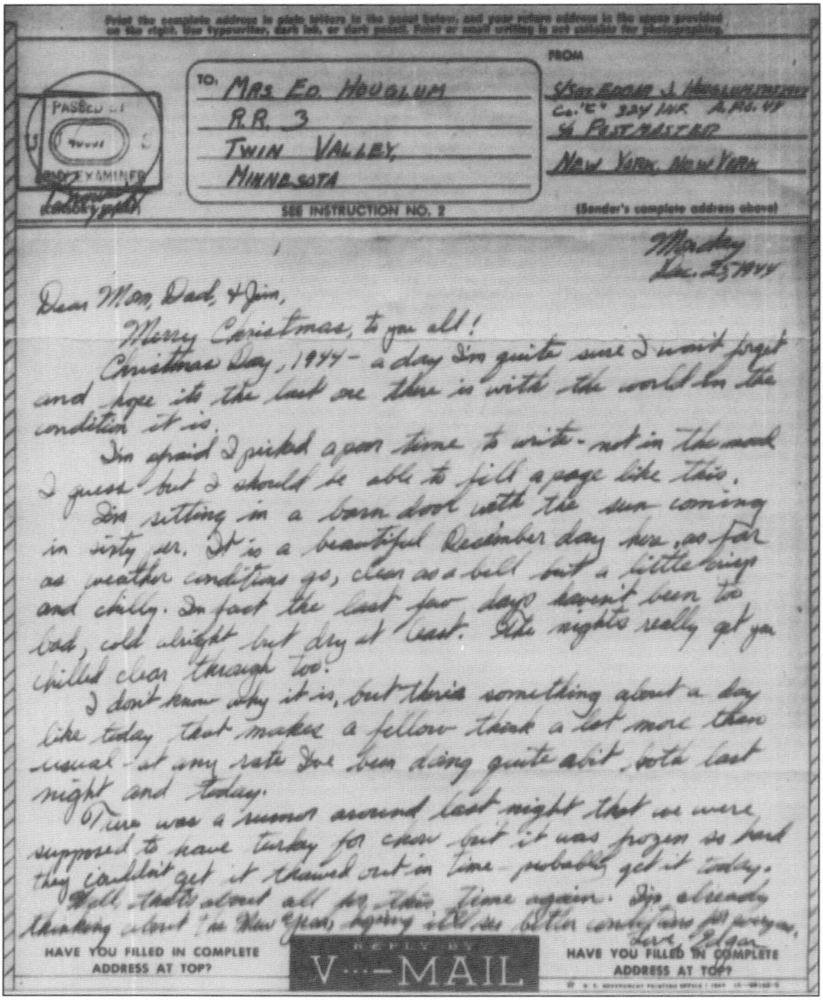

TO: MRS ED. HOUGLUM
R.R. 3
TWIN VALLEY,
MINNESOTA

FROM
[illegible]
Co. "E" [illegible] INF. A.P.O. [illegible]
% POSTMASTER
NEW YORK, NEW YORK

PASSED BY ARMY EXAMINER

SEE INSTRUCTION NO. 2

(Sender's complete address above)

Monday
Dec. 25, 1944

Dear Mom, Dad, & Jim,

Merry Christmas, to you all!

Christmas Day, 1944 – a day I'm quite sure I won't forget and hope its the last one there is with the world in the condition it is.

I'm afraid I picked a poor time to write – not in the mood I guess but I should be able to fill a page like this.

I'm sitting in a barn door with the sun coming in sixty [illegible]. It is a beautiful December day here, as far as weather conditions go, clear as a bell but a little crisp and chilly. In fact the last few days haven't been too bad, cold alright but dry at least. The nights really get you chilled clear through too!

I don't know why it is, but there's something about a day like today that makes a fellow think a lot more than usual – at any rate I've been doing quite a bit, both last night and today.

There was a rumor around last night that we were supposed to have turkey for chow but it was frozen so hard they couldn't get it thawed out in time – probably get it today.

Well, that's about all for this time again. I'm already thinking about the New Year, hoping it'll see better conditions [illegible].

Love, Edgar

HAVE YOU FILLED IN COMPLETE ADDRESS AT TOP?

REPLY BY V···–MAIL

HAVE YOU FILLED IN COMPLETE ADDRESS AT TOP?

A V-mail written on Christmas Day, 1944.

Friday
Dec. 29, 1944

Dear Mom, Dad, & Jim,

I started this quite awhile ago but something else came up so I had to let it go – now I hope I can get it finished. I managed to get a letter off to Clara and one to Joseph earlier this afternoon; yesterday I wrote a couple of other thank you letters – one to the League and one to each of the Ommodt families so now I can rest in peace until I get some more pkgs.

I guess I forgot to tell you that we had a tasty Christmas chow - even though we are where we are. We had turkey and all the fixin's – cranberry sauce, dressing, mashed potatoes, peas, chow chow, pie, even a few nuts and a handful of candy. As far as chow goes, we've been pretty fortunate with two hot meals a day.

Just two more days and a new year begins. I just hope the same that I know lots of others are hoping, that this old world sees a few changes for the better.

Had a letter from Monroe the other day again. Said he['s] been addressing Christmas cards and experimenting with some egg nog – nice work if you can get it and more power to those who can. All again for now so 'bye for now.

Love,
Edgar

[Note: The other people Dad mentioned in this letter are likely my grandfather's sister, Clara Braaten, and brother, Joseph Houglum. The Ommodt families were brothers Bill and Henry; Dad had worked for both, Bill on his farm and Henry at the creamery in Flom. Chow chow was a type of relish.]

The men of the 324th Regiment were unaware that the last few days of December were being used by the German army to prepare for their final big offensive.

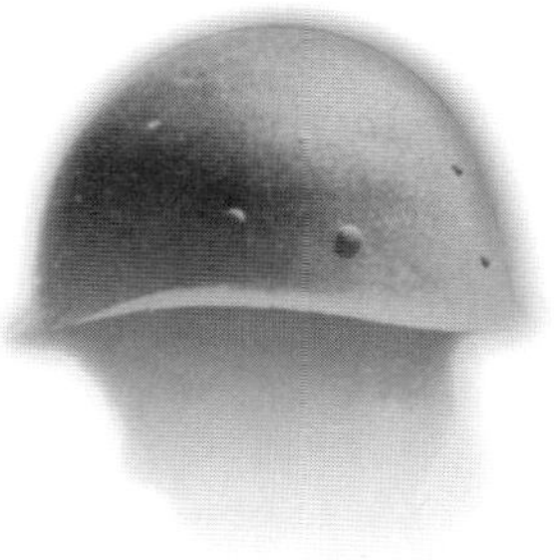

Chapter Nine

Into Germany

By December 1944, the war in Western Europe was not looking good for the German forces. Consequently, Germany planned one more large offensive in an attempt to change the tide of the war in their favor. They planned a surprise attack with a concentrated force along the Allies' line of defense in the Ardennes Mountains near Bastogne, Belgium. This was the Ardennes (or Ardennes-Alsace) Offensive, or generally known as the Battle of the Bulge. The intent of the German plan was to break through the line of defense and surround the Allied forces. The battle began on December 16th. As that battle raged, General Patton was directed to move his Third Army, which had been part of the Allied forces in Alsace-Lorraine, to assist in the Battle of the Bulge. This move left the Seventh Army, which included the 44th Division, along with the French First Army, as the only forces to defend an eighty-four-mile stretch near the French-German border.

As part of the plan to replace the positions of the Third Army as it moved northward to Belgium, the 324th Regiment moved in late December to a position on the Blies River, near Sarreguemines, France. This position was the most western edge of the eighty-four-mile line, which ran east to the German border at the Rhine River and then followed the Rhine south beyond Strasbourg.

When the Third Army moved out of Alsace-Lorraine, the German command realized that an opportunity was available because there was a thin line of defense being held by the Seventh Army. Consequently, Hitler ordered another surprise attack, Operation Northwind (also known as the Second Battle of the Bulge), to begin on New Year's Eve.

Included in this assault was the line held by the 324th Regiment. Success by German troops at this end of the Northwind offensive would allow them to link with other German forces coming around the southern edge of the line, essentially encircling the Allied troops. The German command was convinced that such success by the German forces would bring Patton, or other elements of the U.S. Army, from the battle in Belgium to aid in Alsace-Lorraine, thus ensuring German success in the Ardennes. The details of Operation Northwind, the strategy of the Allied and German forces, and the involvement of each divisional component of the Seventh Army can be found elsewhere.[10,11]

January

Therefore, to start 1945, the 324th Infantry Regiment, along with the rest of the 44th Division, were still in their withdraw position on the France side of the Blies River, just south of Bliesbruck and Frauenberg. The Battle of the Bulge, which had begun mid-December, was about 100 air miles from the position held by the 324th. The consolidation of German troops was in the region of Ardennes (which contained forest and hills in Belgium, Luxembourg, and France) and southward to Alsace.

The objective for the 324th was to hold their position on the south bank of the Blies River and prevent the enemy from taking Bliesbruck and Frauenberg. At midnight on New Year's Eve, the Germans attacked, just as a couple of the Americans were ready to fire some celebratory shots into the air; Operation Northwind was underway. It was a full force attack with artillery in an attempt to break through the thinly stretched lines of the Americans. A break in the front lines would allow the Germans to divide the 44th Division, disrupt the flow of supplies and reinforcements, and give the German army a significant battlefield advantage against the Seventh Army. The fighting was heavy for a few days with each side attempting various maneuvers to outflank the other. Some ground was lost and regained as the number of men killed, wounded, or captured mounted. Time and time again the Americans rebuffed the attempts by the Germans to break through their lines; the intensity of the fighting diminished by the fourth day.[3]

In between the fighting, and as the 324th was holding their ground, Dad found time to write his first letter home of the New Year. Miles away from home and in the midst of cold foxholes and encounters with the enemy, Dad wrote about everything except what he was going through.

January 3, 1945
Wednesday

Dear Mom, Dad, & Jim,

Here's my first letter of the New Year and I see no reason why your not entitle to it. I've got at least two more that should be written tonight if I can make it. One should be sent to Hildur, Bette, and Shirley for the instrument I'm using to write this with – first time I've used it too; the other one goes to Emil Meyers for the package I got today. I got a box of fudge, a little fruit cake, and some candy and peanuts – really good stuff.

Outside of a letter from you a couple of days ago and one from Monroe a little earlier, I haven't had any other letters.

I just happened to think of a couple of little request articles if you can get them for me. I'd like one of those small spiral pocket notebooks – one about three inches wide and four or five inches long. Another thing, which you probably won't be able to get, is a couple of those small flashlight batteries for a penlight – Jim had one once if he remembers. I could also find a place for a couple of standard cells [batteries] *too. I know you can't get them very often but just in case. That's all for now again. I'll try to write another in a few days.*

Love,
Edgar

The 324th Regiment held their positions throughout much of January. They went on patrols to clear the enemy from strategic positions and to obtain reconnaissance information, but mostly they endured the persistent mortar and artillery barrages and the bitter cold (that winter was one of the coldest recorded). Their foxholes were their only protection from weather and the artillery. The German army had high velocity artillery known as the 88's. These were initially designed as anti-air-

Lorraine American Military Cemetery near St. Avold, France is the burial place of over 10,000 American soldiers. It is one of eleven United States cemeteries in France, which are the resting place of over 66,000 World War II American soldiers. (Picture courtesy Catherine Houglum)

craft guns but were able to also fire at a flat trajectory and thus useful as anti-tank weapons. When these big guns were fired into wooded areas, the shells exploded as they hit trees. The explosion caused a barrage of shrapnel fragments to rain from the treetops (treebursts) and caused more casualties than if the shells had exploded on the ground. In an interview on November 3, 2000, regarding his World War II experiences[9] Dad said, *"The Germans used 88's against us. They were deadly... firing at us from long range... very flat trajectory. The treebursts were terrible during bombardment in the forest."* The interviewer noted that even though Dad was describing this experience fifty-five years after its occurrence, he was shaking during the description of the bombardment.

As Dad mentioned in his letter of December 29th, *"... we've been pretty fortunate with two hot meals a day."* The food continued to be in sufficient supply and usually hot for the pre-dawn and after-sunset meals. I remember Dad talking about how the hot chow would be brought close to the front line by the "cooks" and then someone from their company would bring it to the men. The few times that I heard him mention the hot chow on the front line, it was always with a sense of appreciation for that luxury.

In contrast to the hot food, other aspects of their living conditions were miserable. Another notable recollection of Dad's was, *"I remember the cold."*[9] In two of three V-mail letters that Dad wrote home in January, he mentioned the cold and snow.

> *Looks like Old Man Winter has come to stay for awhile – been snowing off and on last night and so far today. Just so it quits soon and doesn't get too cold or I should say much colder.* (January 8)

> *We had another pretty good snow fall last night and this morning accompanied by a fairly stiff breeze, but right now the sun is shining again.* (January 26)

The 44th Division continually held their ground against the German army's attempt to break through the thinly spread line of defense. Near the end of January, it was evident that Operation Northwind was not successful for the German army. However, victory for the Allies was costly with some 18,000 American, and many more French, casualties.

On January 20th, the 44th Division was relieved from their position and received a commendation from General Jacob Devers, commander of the 6th Army Group, for maintaining, *"the integrity of your defense in the face of determined and repeated attacks… "* Their new location was about ten miles south and allowed the men to have showers, haircuts, clean clothes… and heat.

February Promotion

On February 1st, the 324th moved about six miles northeast to the area around Bettviller, France. They relieved the position held by the 71st Regiment, which included farm land and farm buildings. The weather warmed somewhat so rain and mud became problems again, just as they had been in the fall. Also as in the fall, trench foot became a problem and February was deemed "trench foot month." Trench foot is caused by constant exposure of the feet to cold and wet conditions. Sores and blisters can develop as well as fungal infections; in severe cases, amputation is necessary. During World War II tens of thousands of soldiers had to be removed from combat because of trench foot. Therefore, soldiers were supposed to keep a second pair of socks that could be rotated to help prevent the condition. I remember Dad saying that he always kept a second pair of socks inside his uniform to keep them dry and that he would change socks as often as possible to prevent trench foot.

The first half of February was relatively quiet from enemy artillery and mortar fire. During this time, Dad was taken off the front lines to receive a battle field commission, being promoted from staff sergeant to second lieutenant. In many instances, the extra training and education of former ASTP students was put to use by giving them battlefield commissions or other leadership promotions as officers became casualties. These ASTP soldiers had demonstrated their ability to learn quickly in the AST Program and many, like Dad, already had some additional college and/or ROTC training. Some soldiers who were offered battlefield commissions turned them down, but I remember Dad saying that he figured he was being shot at regardless of his rank so he may as well get paid more money for it.

The battlefield commission required some weeks of training. In a V-mail letter home, written at noon on February 7th, he said, *"We've got a pretty good start on our courses now with two and a half days under our belts. So far things aren't too bad, although get*[ting] *back to studying a little again is a bit difficult."* Assuming at least one travel day, he must have left C Company at least by February 4th. Considering he turned twenty-three years old on February 6th, this break from the front lines must have felt like a birthday present to him. In fact, in his February 7th letter he said that he wanted *"... to let you know how I am since I've aged another year as of yesterday. I went over to this Red Cross snack bar, made a couple of trips through the line there for coffee and a couple of French pastries – not bad at all."* In a letter on February 15th Dad said,

> *Well, not many more days, and it looks as though the vacation is over. Its been pretty nice even though spare time has been a little scarce. I guess there isn't much to do around here anyway. This town is just a little berg, and about the only place to spend any time is at the Red*

Cross building I mentioned. Everything there though is jammed full with about a mile long line waiting outside.

To become an officer, Dad had to be discharged from the service as an enlisted man and then re-enlist as an officer. He was honorably discharged on February 16, 1945. He was paid the balance of his wages, which was $121.07. He was commissioned as a second lieutenant on February 17th. Judging from the commissioning document and his February 15th letter, it is possible that February 16th was his last day of this initial officer training and that he went back to his unit on the 16th or 17th. In a letter of February 18th, however, Dad said,

I'm back at the personnel section again – got here this afternoon. I had just finished writing this morning when the word came that we were leaving right after noon chow. Now, I understand, they were notified here that we're to leave here sometime tomorrow, after we get everything straightened out, for a couple more weeks of school – just what kind I can't say, and as to the place, well, that's a bit of a military secret too. It's someplace in the neighborhood of one of France's largest cities.

Part of getting "everything straightened out" evidently was completing his Last Will and Testament, which is dated February 19th. He willed everything to his father. The will was witnessed by three men; one was from his Company C. The document was signed and witnessed in Innswiller, France, so possibly this was the location of his initial officer training courses.

The additional training was a Battlefield Commissioned Officers' Course, which on the certificate of completion states the training was conducted during the period of February 24th to March 16th. The only major city near Dad's location was Paris. I remember Dad saying he was in Paris, so that may have been the location of the training. In addition, the *Combat History of the 324th* indicates that the Artillery Liaison Officer was in Paris during this time, so possibly others traveled with him. There are no V-mails from Dad during this time frame to clarify further.

March

Combat for the 324th did not cease while Dad was obtaining officer's training. They went on patrol after patrol, endured artillery barrages, and mounted the Buchen-Busch Woods attack on February 15th, which continued for three days. Success was seen on the first day with 160 German prisoners and low casualties for the Americans. The Regiment secured their foxholes against artillery barrages during late February and early March, using Bettwiller as their reserve position for showers, clean clothes, and hot meals.

On March 16th, the Division was moved near Willerwald, France (about twelve miles southwest), and put on reserve after 144 consecutive days on the front lines. During their ten days off-line, the soldiers enjoyed showers, hot food, better sleeping conditions, a dental check-up, USO entertainment, music, and Bogart and Bacall in the movie "To Have and Have Not." The time was also used for drills, firing range practice, and other training.

The only V-mail from Dad in March was to his dad; a V-mail birthday card and letter on March 21st. When he wrote my grandfather's birthday V-mail, Dad probably was getting ready to re-join the Regiment. After being out of combat for a few weeks, I'm sure going back to the front line was a dismal thought. But like so many other soldiers, Dad returned to do what he had to do.

> *A day or two more and I'll probably get all the mail that has been piling up during the past weeks. I hope I have sufficient time to read and answer most of it anyway. I hate to admit it, but that's the only thing I'm looking forward to.*

When the 324th moved out of reserve on March 25th, they were transported across the German border to Hertlingshausen. American troops and fighter planes had paved the way along this ninety-four-mile stretch. The Regiment crossed the Rhine on the 27th at Worms, Germany, and, according to the *Combat History of the 324th,* they were the first American infantrymen to reach the Rhine. The first town to be attacked by 324th in this offensive was Vernheim, just across the

Rhine. As a lieutenant, Dad was now a platoon leader and his Company C was placed in front for the attack, but fortunately there was no enemy resistance. The next day they moved southward to the next town, Heddesheim, and met sniper and machine gun fire. After clearing the town of the enemy with tank support, Company C continued southward to Ladenburg where they mopped up the pockets of resistance throughout the town. While Dad's company was taking these towns, other companies of the Regiment were focusing on other towns in the area and meeting with various degrees of enemy resistance. By March 30th, many towns in the surrounding area had been secured by American troops. On March 31st, the Regiment moved over fifty miles north near Zellhausen, Germany, to relieve other units.

April

After clearing the area near Zellhausen, the 324th moved about fifteen miles further north to Gelnhausen, where they remained until April 8th. This is the most northern position the 324th would hold, about twenty-five miles northeast of Frankfurt. They were then moved to Assamstadt, Germany, over fifty air miles to the southeast. From this

The 324th Regiment marches through Ulm, Germany, as liberated Poles rejoice. (Taken from *Combat History 44th Infantry Division*)[8]

point they moved southward across Germany, defeating the German army in small town after small town, sometimes a few yards at a time and sometimes miles at a time. The move began on April 9th and lasted for ten days. The Regiment was spread out to canvas the area of small towns as they moved southeast. They encountered machine gun fire, snipers, mines, and heavy resistance at times. One company would reinforce another as they pushed the German soldiers out of Adolzhausen, Zaisenhausen, Riedback, Kreuzfeld, Kalberback, Sigisweiler, Blaufelden, Speekheim, Heufelwinden, Hausen, Hertershofen, Wiesenbach, Hilgartshausen, and many others.

Soldiers of 324th Regiment crossing the Danube River, April 1945. (Taken from *Combat History 44th Infantry Division*)[8]

Even though the 324th had just finished an exhausting ten days, there was little rest. On April 21st, the 324th continued to move south with orders to reach the Danube River and secure the crossing as quickly as possible. "Fight and keep moving" was the objective. Town after town fell to the Americans as the 324th moved southward towards the Danube, sometimes with house to house fighting to clear the enemy and sometimes meeting the enemy between towns.

On April 23rd, the First Battalion reached the Danube and secured the crossing. Ulm lay to the east on the north side of the Danube, New Ulm on the south side of the river. The First Battalion headed for Ulm and secured the town after several hours of fighting. The next morning, the Second Battalion attacked New Ulm and was able to overpower the enemy; Ulm, New Ulm, and the Danube crossing were in control of the 324th. Eliminating pockets of enemy resistance in the area remained the combat task for several days as the month of April ended. The 324th was less than seventy-five miles from the Austrian border.

Dad's last V-mail home in April was dated the 25th. He had gone through some intense days during April, been wounded, (see next page) moved across many miles of German countryside, and fought in cold, snow, and rain, but was unable to relate any of those experiences to his parents. He mentioned that he had received letters from various people and, of course, mentioned the weather. One thing he did relate is something that reminded him of home. *"We passed through a place the other day and what do you think I saw – lilacs, certainly reminded me of lots of things..."* For sure, home would have been among those "things." Only Dad would know what other specific places and experiences of his boyhood that the sight and smell of lilacs brought rushing through his head; Dad was in Germany, but home was in him.

Silver Star

Out of necessity for victory, heroic efforts by individuals occurred many times during the ten days (April 9-19) of battle as the Regiment pushed southward in Germany; some of these efforts are chronicled in the *Combat History of the 324th.* Many other heroic efforts are not so chronicled, such as men who took aggressive action so that the remainder of their unit could advance more quickly. Dad was awarded the Silver Star for his actions during this time. The citation and the medal didn't catch up to him until he was back in the United States. The citation reads:

> Second Lieutenant EDGAR J. HOUGLUM, 02 006 949, Company C, 324th Infantry. For Gallantry in action on 10 April 1945 in the vicinity of Hilgertshausen, Germany. While leading his platoon in the attack, Lieutenant Houglum received a penetrating wound in the right side from enemy small-arms fire. He was treated by the platoon aid man and advised to go back to the aid station. Lieutenant Houglum, however, returned to his platoon to lead it in the completion of its mission. He then led a half-squad of riflemen in a sharp fire fight to clear a group of houses 150 yards beyond. Lieutenant Houglum's inspirational leadership and aggressive fighting spirit, though wounded, are worthy of high praise. Home address: Twin Valley, Minnesota.

It is likely that many more men deserved than received medals of honor for their acts of valor. During these ten days of battle, the 324th captured 1,737 prisoners and killed or wounded hundreds of others.

The price was not cheap, however, 65 American soldiers dead, 226 wounded. Considering the price of mental agony and physical ordeal that they all endured, recognition with a medal to pin on a uniform seems insufficient.

In an interview[9] about his war experiences, Dad recalled that, *"A number of my men were shot in the head."* Referring to a time when desperation ran high, he also said, *"I dug a foxhole with a spoon from my mess kit during a particularly intense artillery bombardment."* After so many years, these recollections continued to evoke emotion in Dad. Another member of Company C revealed that the pictures in his mind of every battle he was in are as clear today as the day they occurred, and that after recalling such images it takes him a long time to get to sleep at night.[12]

In the eighth episode of *Band of Brothers* (HBO Productions), a mini-series drama based on the true story of the men of Easy Company of the 101 Airborne Division, Private David Webster states:

> I wonder if people back home would ever know what it cost the soldiers to win this war... How could anyone ever know of the price paid by soldiers in terror, agony, and bloodshed if they'd never been to places like Normandy, Bastogne, or Haguenau?

Chapter Ten

The End And The Beginning

May 1945 brought an end to the war but also the beginning of a long hospital recovery and physical rehabilitation period for Dad. By May 1st, rumors were circulating of Hitler's suicide the previous day. During the first week of May, the Allied and German commands were negotiating for Germany's surrender. The speed with which ground was being taken, on German soil no less, provided optimism for the soldiers that the end of the fighting was near. Nonetheless, there were still towns to liberate and an enemy shooting at them. The 324th continued to push southward to the Alps and the Austrian border.

Members of the 324th Infantry Regiment, First Battalion in Imst, Austria, May 1945. (Taken from *Combat History of the 324th Infantry Regiment*)[3]

The Last Letter

At the beginning of May, the Regiment was near Kempten, Germany, about fifteen miles from the Austrian border. The First Battalion was directed to progress through the Fern Pass in the Alps and seize Imst, Austria, which was located about another twenty-five miles beyond the border. They stayed at Lermoos that night, within a few miles of Imst.

Dad had been in combat for months, had taken part in battle after battle, and had escaped without a life-threatening wound. A soldier in combat never knows which day will be his last, nor did Dad have any idea that he would escape death by a slim margin the next day. On the night of May 3rd, Dad wrote a letter home on a sheet of paper, not V-mail. Even though he had been more than a little occupied with fighting a war, he was disgusted with himself for not remembering his cousin's birthday.

Thursday Night
3 May, 1945

Dear Mom, Dad, & Jim,

Just finished reading my mail for today – consisted of two letters from you and one from Donnie. One of yours was dated the 15th & the other the 22nd. In the little addition Monroe put with the one he said he wished I would be more specific about what I do & have done – I wish I could. I'd like to write about everything, for instance where I am right now, where I've been, what I've seen, and where we go in the future but that's out. It seems that any day it doesn't snow now is a rare day. I only hope he doesn't go where I'm afraid he is from the way it sounds.

So Butch doesn't like the mouse trap idea! At least it's one way to keep him away from the curtains, or has he found a way out now?

Yes, I remember the picture you refer to. Keep it around and maybe before too long I'll get a chance to pass a remark or two on the photographer's work.

I was a bit disgusted with myself for forgetting Bette's birthday, but it never entered my head that there were any more birthdays for a while after Jim's. I just wrote them a letter yesterday, too, and didn't even say so much as "happy birthday.["]

I sent another souvenir today and hope it gets their eventually. This time – a good sized German flag – one, along with many others, that will never fly again. Yesterday I sent $30 via PTA [?]. *That's in addition to the $120 allotment that goes home automatically. When you'll get it I don't dare say, but whenever it does, how about buying yourselves some presents? Both Jim & Dad have a birthday present coming, and there's a special day for you, Mom, May 13* [Mother's Day], *which calls for something; so don't write back and say you couldn't find anything you wanted. And don't each of you be satisfied with just a pair of socks or something like that.*

I think somebody is cooking a few eggs, a can or two of boned turkey (obtained through the goodness of our kitchen) down in the kitchen & maybe I ought to have a look.

All for now.

G'night and Love,
Edgar

[Note: Donnie mentioned in the letter was a family friend a few years younger than Dad (see Chapter 4). Donnie wrote to Dad several times while he was in the Army. Butch was the family farm dog.]

Besides the Nazi German flag, presumably the other souvenir alluded to in his letter was a German officer's hat. As children, my siblings and I had seen these two items several times in the storage room at my grandparents' farm. These items were essentially meaningless to me at the time but were of great significance to Dad, and now to me they represent the reason Dad's sacrifice was necessary.

The Last Day

Before dawn on the morning of May 4th, the First Battalion led the way to Imst and was able to move past the town by early morning. As the men moved forward in the wooded steep mountains, A and C Companies encountered the brunt of heavy resistance from small arms and flak guns. With reinforcements from B Company, A and C Companies overcame the resisting forces and moved forward to the next town,

PARIS EDITION

EXTRA THE STARS AND STRIPES EXTRA

Vol. 1—No. 285 1 Fr. 1 Fr. Tuesday, May 8, 1945

VICTORY

Nazis Reveal Surrender To Western Allies, Russia

Germany announced yesterday that it had surrendered unconditionally to the Western Allies and to Soviet Russia.

Headline of *The Stars and Stripes* newspaper, May 8, 1945. Victory was won in Europe but the war in the Pacific was ongoing until VJ Day, August 15, 1945. When World War II was over, the sacrifice for victory included the lives of over 400,000 American soldiers; the price of defeat would have been much greater.

Mils. German officials the next day, under a white flag, knowing that surrender terms were being negotiated to end the war, agreed to a local truce and to pull back to the other side of nearby Landeck.

The Last Casualty

Victory in Europe Day officially came on May 8th when Germany surrendered to the Allied Forces. The 44th Division had a VE-Day parade in Imst with the First Battalion being represented by some members of each of the component companies. But Dad did not make it to Landeck or to the VE-Day parade in Imst. Dad was wounded on May 4th near Imst. According to a letter sent to Dad a year later from his close buddy, Dad was the last casualty in his unit.

May 26, 1946

Dear Edgar,

Well wherever you are I guess you will be very much surprised to hear from me.

Since I saw you last on top of that Mt. down in Austria I have thought of you many times and even in the two or three letters we have written we didn't say much. Hogie! We were pretty close when the "chips" were down over there. We prayed a little and we had some tough times through the weeks and months of fighting. The day you got hit I

Newspaper clipping (source unknown, among Dad's effects) of the 44th Division marching in Victory in Europe Day parade in Imst, Austria, on May 9, 1945; the day after VE-Day.

was over to your right and Hoggie, we left that Kraut up there on that Mt. We also got those flack-guns we were after, or has someone else told you. We left the top of the Mt. after dark and took the town in the valley about 12-o'clock. We didn't loose anyone from that fight and the next day we took Landeck which was pretty large. No fight. The Germans came out in droves and that was the end. In fact Houglum you were in the last battle of the war with "Krauts."

I guess you have been told all that, but I thought I would mention it anyway.

I wish you would write me and let me know how you are getting along and what you plan to do.

I am living in Meridian, Miss., now and I am working for the Toledo scales company. I repair and adjust scales, also install all types of Gra. and market equipment. Don't ask me how I ever got into anything like that for boy I never had an idea I would be doing anything like that. I like being at home every night and having a place where I can live in one place all [the] *time. Be sure and write me all about yourself Hoggie.*

Your Pal,
R.L. Mays.

2100 – 14th St.
Meridian, Miss.
P.S. Be sure and write for I don't want to loose touch with you.

Based on this letter from R.L. Mays, and the fact that the objective for Company C after Imst was to take the town of Mils, Dad was wounded while in the mountains between Imst and Mils, Austria, during the last significant encounter that his company experienced with German soldiers.

When Dad was wounded, he tried to apply a tourniquet to his leg but was not able to stop the bleeding and quickly became weak from the rapid loss of blood. What goes through a person's mind when a critical situation like that suddenly occurs? Maybe Dad thought of Thora Thompson's words, *"by trusting in the Lord he will carry you thru my boy."* I heard Dad comment more than once that if the medic had not been close behind him, he would not have survived. After being treated by the medic, and as his platoon and Company C continued toward their objective, Dad was moved to the Battalion Aid Station.

May 4, 1945, was a Friday, so my grandparents were probably going about their normal daily chores on that day. They certainly didn't know at that time how close they came to losing their middle son. In fact, as they heard the news of Germany's surrender on May 8th, they were probably relieved. I cannot imagine the emotional stress that hit them when they received the news from the Army regarding Dad being seriously wounded. Put yourself in their place, with no telephone, no text messaging, and no email, but you receive a Western Union message like they did on May 17th that read as follows:

Mrs Alma O Houglum
RR 3 Twin Valley, Minn.

The secretary of war desires me to express his deep regret that your son 2 Lt Houglum Edgar J was seriously wounded in Austria 04 May 45 period hospital sending you new address and further information period unless such new address has been received address mail for him quote rank name serial number (hospitalized) central postal directory APO 640 C/O Postmaster New York, New York unquote

Since my grandparents did not have a phone, the telegram was one means of being sure that they would receive the news. Dad's brother, Jim, recalls that Ole Vange, a neighbor to the south of the farm, had a telephone and that he also received the same message by phone for him to relay to my grandparents. Whether by phone or Western Union telegram, it is a message no one wants to receive and probably most parents and spouses of those in combat fear they will. In the absence of any quick means of communication, the wait for additional word must have riddled the days with anxiety and emotional stress.

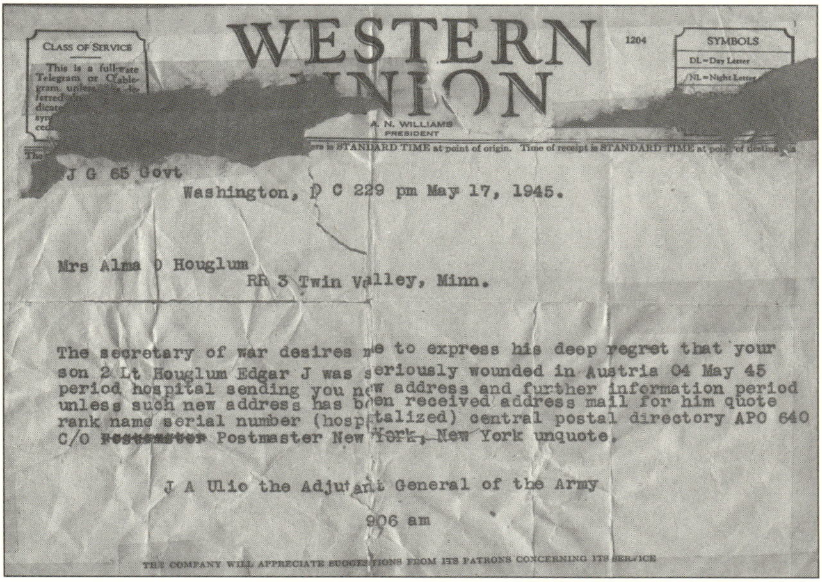
CLASS OF SERVICE
This is a full-rate Telegram or Cable-gram unless ...

WESTERN UNION
A. N. WILLIAMS PRESIDENT
1204
SYMBOLS
DL=Day Letter
NL=Night Letter

... is STANDARD TIME at point of origin. Time of receipt is STANDARD TIME at point of destination

J G 65 Govt
Washington, D C 229 pm May 17, 1945.

Mrs Alma O Houglum
RR 3 Twin Valley, Minn.

The secretary of war desires me to express his deep regret that your son 2 Lt Houglum Edgar J was seriously wounded in Austria 04 May 45 period hospital sending you new address and further information period unless such new address has been received address mail for him quote rank name serial number (hospitalized) central postal directory APO 640 C/O ~~Postmaster~~ Postmaster New ~~York,~~ New York unquote.

J A Ulio the Adjutant General of the Army

906 am

THE COMPANY WILL APPRECIATE SUGGESTIONS FROM ITS PATRONS CONCERNING ITS SERVICE

The telegram sent to my grandmother from the Army, May 17, 1945.

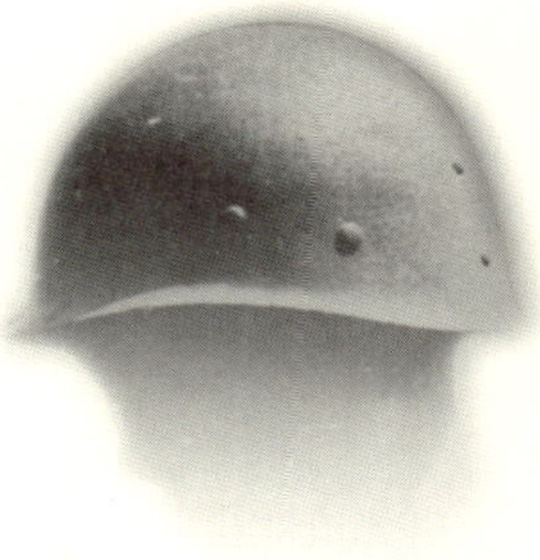

Chapter Eleven

The Road To Recovery Leads Home

The initial Western Union message to my grandparents informing them that Dad had been seriously wounded was dated May 17, 1945. The next message received was from the Protestant chaplain; it was dated May 22nd, so probably arrived about a week after the first notification of Dad's critical condition. After receiving this letter, my grandparents no doubt remained very concerned about Dad, but the chaplain provided some optimism that must certainly have provided comfort. Even as a young adult, I was completely oblivious that these events had occurred and thus never once had a thought to ask my grandmother any questions regarding them. Continuing with daily tasks must have been a challenge for my grandparents during the week or so of uncertainty until the chaplain's typed letter arrived.

4355 U.S. ARMY HOSPITAL PLANT
APO 513 Postmaster NYC, NY
22 May 1945

Mrs Alma Houglum,
Twin Valley, Route 3,
Minnesota

Dear Mrs Houglum,

The Commanding Officer of this Hospital has requested me to write to you concerning your son, 2D Lt Edgar J Houglum, ASN

0-2006949, of Company C, 324th Infantry, 44th Division, who is now a patient in this Hospital.

As you have been informed, he was a battle casualty and has a perforated wound in his left thigh. Though now in a serious condition, the ward Surgeon says the outlook for his recovery is good. He was able to give us information needed to reach you. He is receiving the best care from surgeons, physicians, and technicians skilled in their work. The Nurses are also doing everything they can, by careful attention and nursing for his comfort and recovery.

I have seen him and talked with him about you and he wants you to know that he is feeling better. Being a Protestant Chaplain, I shall continue to minister to him as a Protestant patient in any way that I can.

It is requested that you do not write to the Commanding Officer of the Hospital, in response to this letter, as all the available information at this time is contained in this letter. You will receive further letters at semi-monthly intervals as long as your sons' condition is considered serious. But personally, I shall be glad to correspond with you at any time concerning him.

I assure you of my regret of having to send bad news to you, but do not be too much disturbed, for progress has been made and the outlook is good. I shall see him often and do what I can for him, both in ministration and prayer.

Sincerely, Yours in Christ,
C.O. Boatman [signature]
C.O. BOATMAN,
Protestant Chaplain

The Damage

According to Dad's medical history as recorded in the Disposition Board Proceedings of May 23, 1947, the bullet from small arms fire penetrated through Dad's left thigh, entering postero-laterally and exiting antero-medially. It severed the femoral artery and vein and caused paralysis of the peroneal and saphenous nerves, causing immediate profuse bleeding and paralysis of the left leg. From the Battalion Aid

Station, Dad was transported to the 127th Evac Hospital in Germany where the wounds were cleaned and debrided and the femoral vein and artery were ligated. He was then transferred to the 99th General Hospital in Verdun, France, about May 10th and the wound was closed. Unfortunately the vessels began hemorrhaging and the wound was re-opened and the vessels ligated again. On June 26th, he was transferred to the 90th General Hospital in Bar-le-Duc, France, and then in July transferred to the 1st Air Evac Hospital at Paris. Dad was flown back to the United States and was admitted as a patient on July 17, 1945, at O'Reilly General Hospital, Springfield, Missouri, until March 1946.

On May 24th, Dad was feeling well enough to write a V-mail home.

24 May 45
VERDUN

Dear Mom, Dad, & Jim,

No doubt by this time you've had several notifications of what happened. I know you've been waiting for a letter from me too, but I haven't felt quite up to it. The nurse came in with this V-mail and asked me how long it had been since I had written – she addressed it for me.

As you see, I'm in a hospital in Verdun. As yet I've been on my back ever since I got here, with the exception of a few hours this morning and one other day.

I was hit the 4th near the the[sic] *town of Imst, Austria. Coming back here I had my first plane ride although I couldn't see from where I was. Boy, I've had more needles stuck in me now than a pin cushion. My wound is just above the left knee, but it sort of raised cane inside with the artery, vein, & nerve, and that's what's giving me all the pain. The doctor told me the other day that as soon as I could stand the trip I'd be going back to the states. Hope you can read this. Bye for now.*

Love,
Edgar

My grandparents received two additional letters from chaplains, each with much better news than the previous one. Among the few statements I heard Dad say regarding his military experience was that

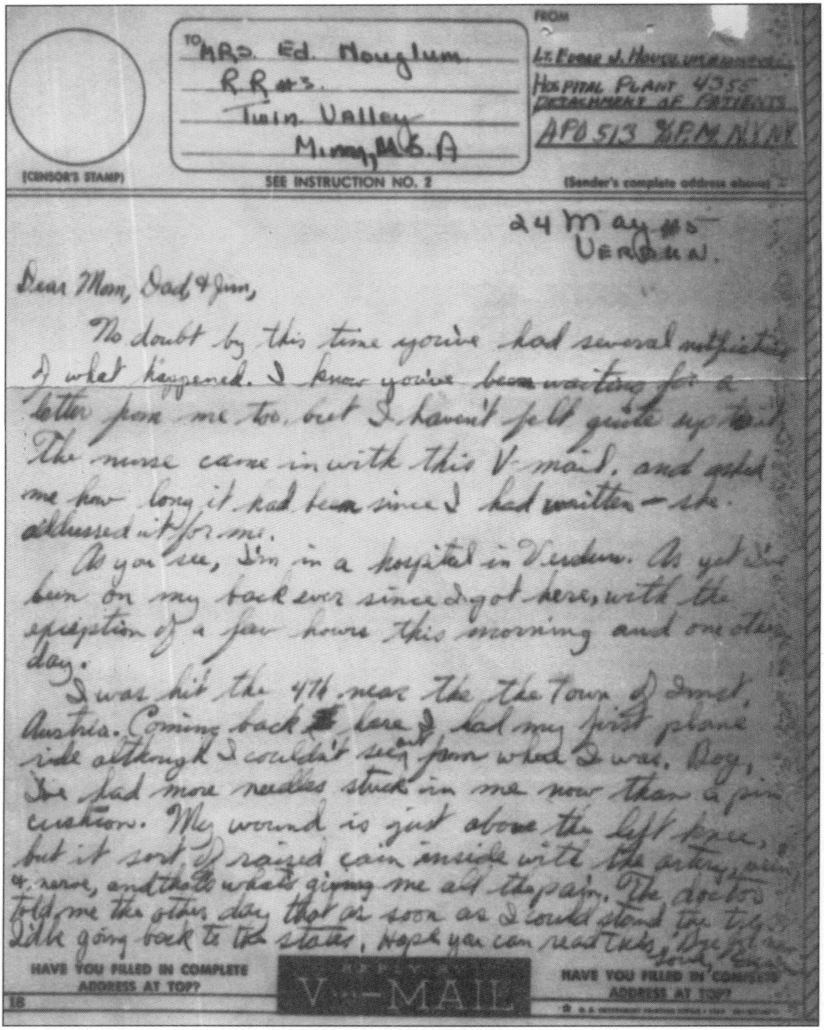
TO MRS. Ed. Houglum
R.R #3.
Twin Valley
Minn, U.S.A

FROM
Lt. [illegible] J. Houglum
Hospital Plant 4355
Detachment of Patients
APO 513 % P.M. N.Y. N.Y.

(CENSOR'S STAMP)
SEE INSTRUCTION NO. 2
(Sender's complete address above)

24 May 45
Verdun.

Dear Mom, Dad & Jim,

No doubt by this time you've had several notifications of what happened. I know you've been waiting for a letter from me too, but I haven't felt quite up to it. The nurse came in with this V-mail, and asked me how long it had been since I had written — she addressed it for me.

As you see, I'm in a hospital in Verdun. As yet I've been on my back ever since I got here, with the exception of a few hours this morning and one other day.

I was hit the 4th near the the town of Imst, Austria. Coming back here I had my first plane ride although I couldn't see out from where I was. Boy, I've had more needles stuck in me now than a pin cushion. My wound is just above the left knee, but it sort of raised cain inside with the artery, vein & nerve, and that's what's giving me all the pain. The doctor told me the other day that as soon as I could stand the trip I'd be going back to the states. Hope you can read this. [illegible] Love, [illegible]

HAVE YOU FILLED IN COMPLETE ADDRESS AT TOP?
REPLY BY V—MAIL
HAVE YOU FILLED IN COMPLETE ADDRESS AT TOP?

The first V-mail Dad wrote after being wounded, May 24, 1945.

he would not let the medical staff resort to amputating his leg. This typed letter from Chaplain Boatman mentions that the outlook is good that amputation will not be necessary.

OFFICE OF THE PROTESTANT CHAPLAIN
99th Gen. Hosp. A.P.O. 513
c/o Postmaster N.Y., N.Y.
14 June '45

Mr. And Mrs. Edward Houglum
Twin Valley Minnesota

Dear Mr. and Mrs Houglum,

Your letter of thanks and inquiry received, and I hasten to say that it was only my duty to be the bearer of bad news, and at the time I wrote I was not feeling too optimistic about the rapid recovery of your son, and his recovery has been slow, but sure, as he has been taken off the seriously ill list, some time ago.

As I promised to do I have visited with him many times and in addition to that, an assistant Chaplain, who is a Lutheran, has seen him and administered Holy Communion. We have also supplied him with reading matter and tried in other ways to be of service to him. The outlook for a complete recovery without the loss of even a part of his limb, is now seemingly assured and he is in good spirits over it all. I feel that you need have no further fears as to the final outcome of it all, and there is a possibility that he may be back in the States in the not too distant future, for at least a Leave of Absence, if not otherwise.

We join you in praying that all will be well and that he shall soon be returned to you. We assure you that we shall be glad to do what we can for his comfort and progress. As you are hearing from him direct now, we will not write you again, unless there should be the unexpected.

Sincerely, Yours-in Christ.
C.O. Boatman [signature]
Chaplain C.O. Boatman
Protestant Chaplain

29 June 1945

Dear Mrs. Houglum,

On Tuesday of this week your son, Edgar, was evacuated from this hospital, since this unit is in the process of closing. You will undoubtedly be hearing from him soon from his new address.

I believe I am able to report now that his present condition is very favorable. During the past seven weeks he has come a long way on the road to recovery. For two days prior to his leaving he was able to be about in a wheelchair and on the very day of his departure it was planned to take him outside so that he could watch a baseball game.

I wish you could have heard the comments from doctors, nurses, and enlisted men who attended him, when they learned that Edgar was to be evacuated. They were truly sorry to see him leave and in all sincerity said that he was the best patient the 99th has had. Having had the occasion to be with him many times and for long periods, I share in their opinion.

It is the present policy of the War Department to return the war wounded to the states as soon as their condition allows them to be moved. I feel confident that Edgar will be on his way back in a short time.

Sincerely yours,
Carl R. Eggers [signature]
Chaplain (Luth) U.S. Army

The final V-mail from Dad was written from Paris as he was waiting to be airlifted to the United States. Judging from this letter, there were other letters written to home that were not among Dad's letters saved by my grandparents.

Paris
9 July, 1945

Dear Mom, Dad, & Jim,

I hadn't figured on being here long enough so I'd have to write more than one letter but its beginning to look otherwise. I was under the impression that one or two, maybe three days at the most was as long as any one stayed here – not so, one fellow has been here nineteen days now. Most of the officers here – or at least a good percentage – are laid up with broken legs suffered in jeep wrecks. Since all fractures are gong to the States, that's where they've headed.

Today I was outside for nearly three hours, the sun certainly felt good for a change. This place used to be a school and the grounds are quite large and with the P.W.'s & civilian labor, they've really fixed it up – supposed to be "show-spot" of Paris or E.T.O. [European Theatre of Operation]

P.X. rations today, more candy & gum – no beer this time. All for now.

Goodnight. Love,
Edgar

After Dad's wound was cleaned and the bleeding stopped in France, a cast was put on his leg and his leg rested on his left heel. Since the nerve in that leg had been severed by the bullet, Dad had no pain sensation and thus couldn't feel that he had developed a severe pressure sore on the left heel. This pressure sore contributed to his lengthy stay in the hospital. When he was transferred to O'Reilly General Hospital in July, Dad received penicillin for the pressure sore as well as physical therapy and exercises. However, problems with the heel persisted and a chunk of dead or infected tissue was removed, leaving a substantially diminished heel.

Dad recovering at O'Reilly General Hospital, Springfield, Missouri, c. fall 1945.

In October, the slow process of a full thickness graft was begun to replace the excised tissue on the heel. Tissue from Dad's right thigh was used to fill the void in his left heel. To accomplish this, Dad had to lie with his left heel on his right thigh as the tissue was gradually removed from the thigh, stitched to the heel, and then slowly grew attached to the heel; in essence, his heel was sown to his thigh during this process. The surgery was considered finished about December 17, 1945.

Although Dad didn't make it home for Christmas in 1945, his eventual return home was more assured now than it had been a year earlier when he had written from the battlefield in France. Dad wrote the following on a Christmas card:

15 December, 1945

Dear Mom, Dad, & Jim,

I don't know if its exactly the proper thing to do – write on Xmas cards but I'm doing it anyway. Wrote a little on one to Hildur and one to Thelma. I finally got around to sending those pictures to Hildur.

Well, today I was up in a wheelchair and saw a movie in the ward. Oh, yesterday I talked one of the ward boys into helping [me] *into the bathroom again so now I hope I'm through with bed pans for good. Its been kind of hard to have had a private bath for the past three weeks and not be able to use it. I sat on a chair yesterday and realized how much weight I had lost – hardest chair I ever sat on! My appetite seems to be on the up & up again though so it shouldn't be too long before some of the padding comes back. The stiffness is coming out of the old pins pretty well again – still kind of "neak in the wees" though, I found out today.*

That show I mentioned we had today turned out to be pretty good "Pillar to Post" – comedy. Last night some U.S.O. show put on a little show up here too – quite short but a change.

I learned a few of the high points of the game called penuckle [pinochle] *last night. A couple of the nurses were the teachers – I'll admit I got beat.*

I still haven't had any suggestions for your Christmas presents.

Finish for now.

Love,
Edgar

Dad remained at O'Reilly General until he was transferred to the Convalescent Annex of Percy Jones General Hospital in Battle Creek, Michigan; an Army hospital near Fort Custer which specialized in neurosurgery, plastic surgery and the fitting of artificial limbs. He was admitted to this hospital on March 4, 1946. Some aspects of his physical exam upon admission that were noted in the medical report included a well-healed bullet entrance wound on the side of the left thigh and a ten-inch scar on the inside surface of the leg from the surgery. There was moderate atrophy of the lower portion of the left leg, and Dad was wearing a drop foot brace on the left foot because the severed nerve prevented him from lifting his foot while walking. On March 14th the neurosurgical consultant recommended Dad for sixty-day convalescent leave followed by re-examination. What great news this must have been; after nearly a year in various hospitals, Dad could head back home on leave!

Heading Home

A letter from a fellow patient who was still at O'Reilly General Hospital, Lt. Joseph P. Chap mentioned hearing of Dad's first leave.

> *May 31, 1946*
>
> *Dear Ed,*
>
> *I received your most welcome letter just before I left on leave. When I returned Shirley told me that you too had just returned from your first sick leave. At last you got home & I'll bet you had a lot to do. I'm an old hand at sick leave & I recall how busy I was on my first.*

In his letter, Lt. Chap told Dad about how his wounds are progressing and also that he just became a father on May 12th to a baby boy, seven pounds, ten ounces. Lt. Chap ended the letter with,

> *I guess I blew my top for awhile now how about some word from you. Please write & this time an answer will come soon. I was a little too busy for letters as you can read. I remain*
>
> *Your buddy,*
>
> *Joe*

Dad's official orders state that he was to receive sixty days sick leave beginning on or about March 22nd. Thus, Dad probably returned home during the last week or so of March 1946. At last, the lion's share of his sacrifice for his country was over. Yes, he would limp the rest of his life; he would stumble on cracks in the side walk, and sometimes fall on his face because he would never be able to lift his left foot up as he brought the leg forward. Yet the physical exhaustion of combat day after day, the tension of going on patrols, the fright of hearing German artillery overhead, and life in cold, wet foxholes was over.

On his route home, I wonder if Dad thought of all of his buddies who were never going to make their trip home. Dad was a decorated soldier, but knowing him, I'll bet he gave thought to how small his sacrifice was in comparison to that of many of his comrades still in hospitals or those who would never return from France. As he arrived in the farm yard for the first time, I wonder if the previous eighteen months seemed like a dream from which he was finally awaking to find himself right back where he started–home.

The first morning our daughter was back after being deployed to the Middle East for a few months during the beginning of the second Gulf War, she recounts that as she awoke that first morning the whole experience felt like a dream, in part because everything at home had remained just as she had left it. I don't know what was going through Dad's mind and the emotions he was experiencing as he approached home in March 1946, but it was not likely an experience he would ever forget.

As for my grandparents, to know that they came within seconds of losing one of their sons must have made their reunion with him all the more precious. I'm sure they were thankful that their son was home. Was it the prayers of Dad and his foxhole buddy, R.L., and of family and friends that ensured the medic was right behind Dad when his vein and artery were severed by the bullet?

After Dad's sixty days of leave, he returned to Percy Jones General Hospital for another evaluation on June 10th. Again he was recommended for convalescent leave, this time for ninety days, presumably to give more time for the healing process before returning to active duty. It was determined that he was past the stage where physical therapy and electro stimulation would be needed. Therefore, his continuous stay in the hospital wasn't necessary, but additional healing time was.

So Dad was able to return home again for an extended stay. Of course there are no letters during these convalescent leaves, but no doubt Dad was kept busy with visiting friends and relatives and enjoying the simple pleasures of peace: hot meals, a soft bed, a warm house, and the freedom to roam outdoors without explosions or gunfire. Most of us will never experience the tragedies and hardships of being on the frontline of war, nor can we imagine the enhanced value that life's simple pleasures hold after these experiences. I wish I would have asked Dad about his feelings during these convalescent leaves and what was most important to him at that time as compared to before the war. I wonder if his freedom to enjoy these simple pleasures would be among the top of the list.

Dad visiting his Aunt Emma, her daughters and grandchildren in International Falls, April 1946.

More Hospitals

After Dad's extended sick leave, I expect that it was difficult for my grandparents to see him leave again. At least they knew he was returning to a hospital, not a foxhole. My grandmother wrote to him, postmarked October 17, 1946, just to keep in touch. Interestingly she mentioned that people were able to get meat again.

Wed. Eve.

Dear Edgar,

Your letter here today also from Jim. So good to hear. I washed this morning. This P.M we were to Apsahls funeral in Am Sure could have filled church three times. My what a crowd. Were upstairs in basement and halls and little rooms in front of church, all over.

Dad hauled 3 loads of hay today besides.

Tonite we got company. Monroe came out with Selvina. She had been at Pipestone & Mpls and decided to stop off here hoping Monroe was in Waubun so she'd have a way to get out. She found their place alright, asked at bus Depot. Monroe & Thelma & Bruce were out last nite, Monroe went to choir practise.

Forgot to tell you about cattle Dad sold last week. Got about 15¢ a lb for all the steers. Said before he got check, he should get 12. ¢ so guess he was satisfied couple more going soon I guess. Spose people are getting meat now the way stock reports sound. I just got upstairs cleaned up in time for company. I kept thinking about Stella coming all yesterday when cleaning and here Sel pops up.

No weather change much. Sun did shine little bit this forenoon but cloudy again now. Keep on till we get snow I spose. Fri eve we have our aid sale. Hope its nice then.

Had announcement card from Joyce Meyer yesterday. Baby boy there, Richard Merlyn.

Dad had trouble with tractor yesterday & day before but got it going again yesterday P.M. Sun[day] *he worked on car coz that troubled but goes fine again now. Now I better call this enuff for this time. Hoping all goes fine & be thinking about my boys.*

Love,
Dad & Mom

In her October 17th letter, my grandmother included the letter that Jim had sent her. Jim enlisted in the Army earlier that month. He served until January 1948 and was part of the occupation troops in Italy.

Ft. Belvoir, Va.
Sat. nite

Dear Folks,

We finally got here & now have an address. Got in here this morning – were on a si ding most of last nite in Richmond, Va. Left Ft. Sheri-

dan about 3 P.M. Thurs. When we got thru Chicago it was dark (gets dark earlier here than at home) Woke up in Columbus, Ohio. Went thru part of Ky. & Va. Thru the Alleghenie Mts. All day yesterday – following a river – all the towns were coal mining towns – This was really the most beautiful scenery I've ever seen. Really enjoyed the trip – had Pullman sleepers too. The fellow from N.D. is upstairs in the same barracks. Another swell guy (whose pencil I'm using now) is with me in the bottom – from St. James, Minn. One fellow here is from Texas – lot from Missouri – one from Michigan – some from Wisconsin.

It rained here tonight when we were having chow – really poured. Pretty nice camp here – green grass yet – but we're restricted for 2 weeks to our area. Basic is 8 weeks but probably won't start for a week or so. This is definetly the army engineers.

Chow has been pretty good but not enough especially bread – every body here is always hungry. Got our rifles today – looks pretty rugged – I can't see myself taking a gun apart. In our clothing issue we got an E.T.O. Jacket instead of the old blouse. Thats the short Eisenhower one - also got the field jacket like Monroes.

A little while ago there were arguments about the best states. Tex really got it as he's alone from Texas.

Better send me Edgars address in case I get time I'll write to him.

Everybody seems to be in bed so guess I'll quit. Army life still isn't too bad.

Love,
Jim

P.t. James E. Houglum
Co. C. 5th BN E.T.C.
1st Platoon
Fort Belvoir, Va.

Plan on going to church tomorrow, too.
We're about 20-30 miles from Washington D.C.

Dad was seen by the neurosurgeon again at Percy Jones on September 13th. He met with the Army Disposition Board on October 23rd, and the Army Retiring Board for Officers on November 13th. His entire medical history was again reviewed at these meetings. The proceedings from these meetings state that Dad was experiencing numbness in parts of his left leg and foot with some discomfort with weather changes or lower temperature, and that his leg tired quite easily when he walked or stood for any length of time. Paralysis of the left saphenous nerve was complete but sensory response was improving. The boards determined that Dad was temporarily incapacitated for active military service but that a reevaluation should be conducted in six months.

On October 16th, Dad was promoted to first lieutenant, but he was not permitted to return to active duty. Dad's orders indicate that sick leave was granted on or about November 16th for thirty days, which was extended for another thirty days on December 13th. Considering that two years earlier, Christmas 1944, was a low point for Dad and his buddies because they were recovering from a battle with the German army that sent the 324th Regiment in retreat, being home in 1946 must have seemed like a slice of heaven. The contrast from Christmas 1944 in France and 1945 in the hospital, to being home in 1946 couldn't have been more stark, and I doubt that realization escaped him.

Dad's recovery continued at Percy Jones General Hospital until February 1947 when he was transferred for neurosurgery evaluation at Tilton General Hospital at Fort Dix, New Jersey. No surgery was conducted at Tilton General to improve Dad's ability to move his foot, in part because he had gained sensory perception in his left leg and the physicians were concerned that exploratory surgery to investigate one nerve may risk losing the feeling he had re-gained from the other nerves.

He was only at Fort Dix until April, but during that time he was able to see some sites in New York City as part of the organized outings that were available to ambulatory patients. Dad went to the New York Botanical Garden, a St. Patrick's Day celebration, the Waldorf Astoria, and the quarter finals basketball games of the National Invitational Tournament at Madison Square Garden. He also saw Broadway plays at The Booth Theatre, "Tenting Tonight;" The Empire Theatre, "O Mistress Mine;" and the St. James Theatre, "Oklahoma!" A veteran's organization called The 52 Association, whose motto was "the wounded shall never be forgotten," arranged parties at military hospitals; their newsletter indicates one was scheduled for Tilton Hospital for March 12th.

I remember Dad talking about seeing "Oklahoma" and the general sites of New York City, such as Times Square. Close proximity to the New York social and cultural life, plus the fact that he was ambulatory, allowed him to enjoy his stay at Tilton General Hospital. After sixty years, he still had memorabilia from all these events.

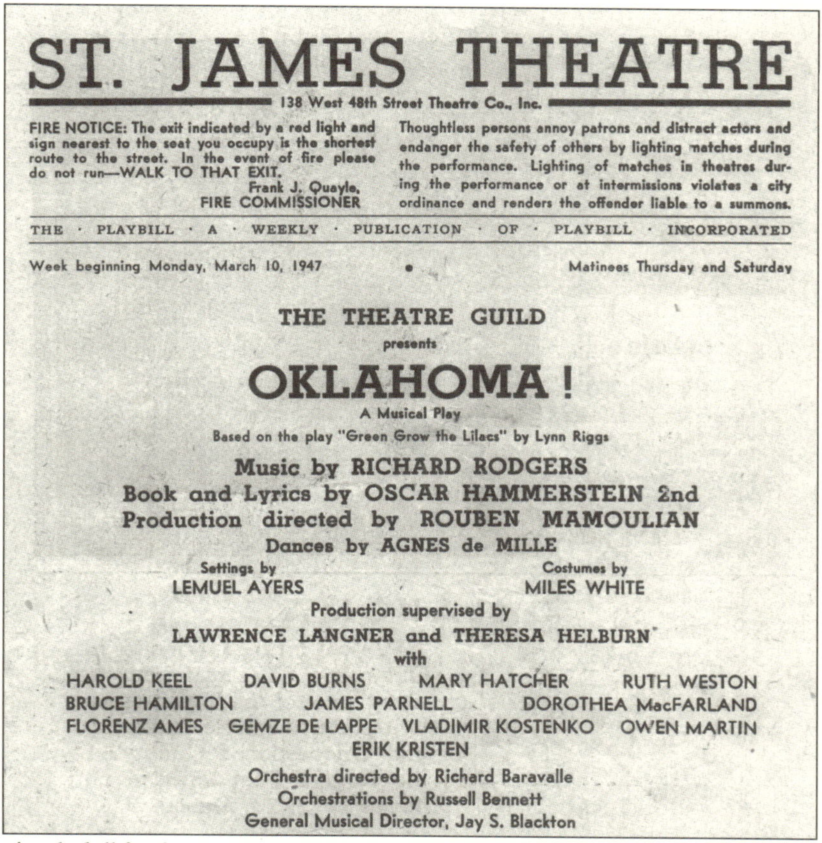

ST. JAMES THEATRE

138 West 48th Street Theatre Co., Inc.

FIRE NOTICE: The exit indicated by a red light and sign nearest to the seat you occupy is the shortest route to the street. In the event of fire please do not run—WALK TO THAT EXIT.
Frank J. Quayle,
FIRE COMMISSIONER

Thoughtless persons annoy patrons and distract actors and endanger the safety of others by lighting matches during the performance. Lighting of matches in theatres during the performance or at intermissions violates a city ordinance and renders the offender liable to a summons.

THE · PLAYBILL · A · WEEKLY · PUBLICATION · OF · PLAYBILL · INCORPORATED

Week beginning Monday, March 10, 1947 • Matinees Thursday and Saturday

THE THEATRE GUILD
presents
OKLAHOMA!
A Musical Play
Based on the play "Green Grow the Lilacs" by Lynn Riggs
Music by RICHARD RODGERS
Book and Lyrics by OSCAR HAMMERSTEIN 2nd
Production directed by ROUBEN MAMOULIAN
Dances by AGNES de MILLE
Settings by LEMUEL AYERS
Costumes by MILES WHITE
Production supervised by
LAWRENCE LANGNER and THERESA HELBURN
with
HAROLD KEEL DAVID BURNS MARY HATCHER RUTH WESTON
BRUCE HAMILTON JAMES PARNELL DOROTHEA MacFARLAND
FLORENZ AMES GEMZE DE LAPPE VLADIMIR KOSTENKO OWEN MARTIN
ERIK KRISTEN
Orchestra directed by Richard Baravalle
Orchestrations by Russell Bennett
General Musical Director, Jay S. Blackton

The playbill for the Broadway musical, "Oklahoma." According to Dad's ticket, he saw the matinee performance on March 15, 1947, and sat in the balcony in seat N5. The ticket price was $1.80.

Physically Unfit to Serve

After his short stay at Fort Dix, Dad traveled back to Michigan and was re-admitted to Percy Jones General Hospital on April 27th. On May 23rd, the Disposition Board met again to discuss Dad's medical file and to determine his ability to return to active duty. For posterity sake, included here is the physical examination results as recorded in the Disposition Board's report:

> Patient has almost complete absence of dorsi-flexion of the left foot and with a minimal ability of plantar flexion of the foot. There is no dorsi-flexion of the left great toe. There is a mild ankylosis of the left ankle joint as well as ankylosis of the first metacarpal phalangeal joint. The long flexor hallious is functioning, however, the short is not. Circumference of the right thigh 10" above the inferior patellar border 21" and corresponding level on the left thigh 20½." Circumference of the right calf 6" below patella border, 15" corresponding level on the left, calf 14½." So far, neurological exam motor function, left leg, is intact except as mentioned above. Sensory function is intact, except for an area of loss of the epicritis sensation in the medial aspect, proximal two-thirds of the left leg and for an area on the anterior surface of the right thigh, in both upper and lower extremities. Babinskis is not present. Skin on the left thigh, distal third, lateral aspect, there is a small wound of entrance and on the medial aspect, distal third, there is a long oblique, well healed surgical scar originating on the anterior surfaces of the left thigh, mid portion and ending in the medial aspect of the left popliteal space. Patient is able to walk on toes. When attempts to walk on heals, is unable to dorsiflex the left foot.
>
> Final impression – Complete paralysis of the saphenous nerve on the left and paralysis of the peroneal nerve on the left...
>
> Chest plate on 28 April 1947 was essentially negative. X-ray 8 May 1947, insofar as the left femur and left ankle joint, shows an old healed fracture of the left femur at the junction of middle and distal third of the bone with a minimal deformity of the shaft.

> …patient has been seen in consultation by the Orthopedic Services in regards to the patient's complaint of a grating in his knee and occasional pain in knee. It was the opinion and recommendation of the Orthopedist that the symptoms relative to the knee joint may be due to a chondromalacia of the patella. However, there was no orthopedic treatment indicated at this time…

The decision of the Disposition Board was that Dad should meet with the Army Retiring Board, which he did on June 12th. Again Dad's medical history was reviewed in detail, with some additional attention given to the "twinging" pain in his left knee which he had experienced since the fall of the previous year, and his inability to stand for an extended period. The recommendation of the board was that because of Dad's physical injuries sustained as a result of being wounded on May 4, 1945, he was "unfit for any type of military service." The Board advised him of his right to apply for military pension. The Army was satisfied that they had done what they could to treat Dad's wounds and that healing was never going to be satisfactory to keep Dad on active duty.

The medical exams and lab tests that Dad had undergone over and over were now finally completed. There would be no more meetings with specialists and no more shuttling from one hospital to another. Dad had spent nearly a year in the hospital immediately after being wounded, and then assigned to one hospital or another for over a year for rehabilitation, re-examination, and re-assessment of his progress. The final action on the Board's recommendation needed to be made by the War Department. In the meantime, Dad was granted thirty days of sick leave on June 6th, which was followed by an extension of another thirty days.

The War Department accepted the recommendation of the Army Retiring Board. Dad was separated from the Army on September 16, 1947. His Army retirement pay was set at $157.50 per month. He had given over four years to his country; the rest of his life was his own. I wonder if he celebrated.

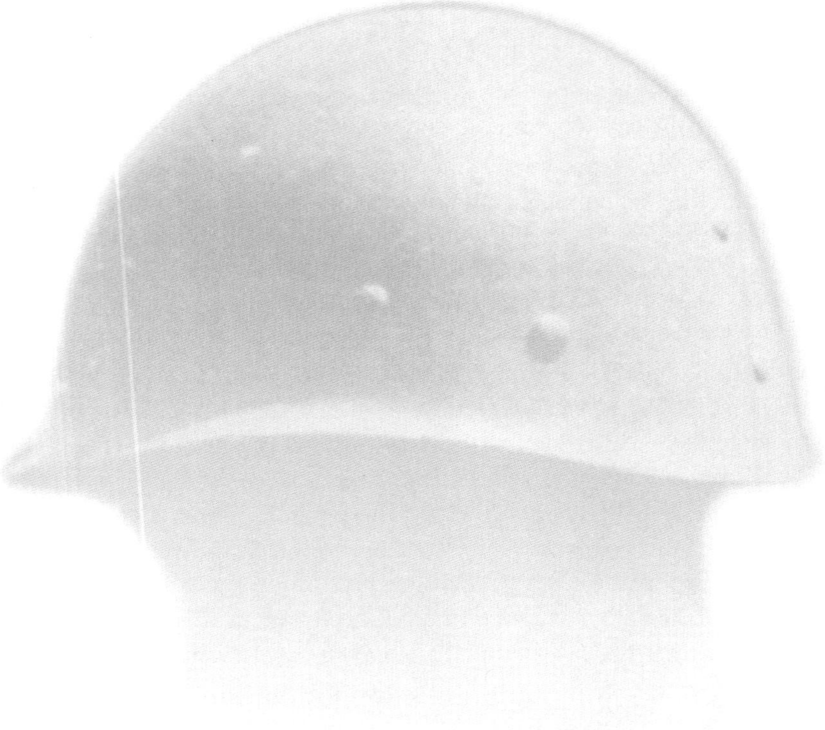

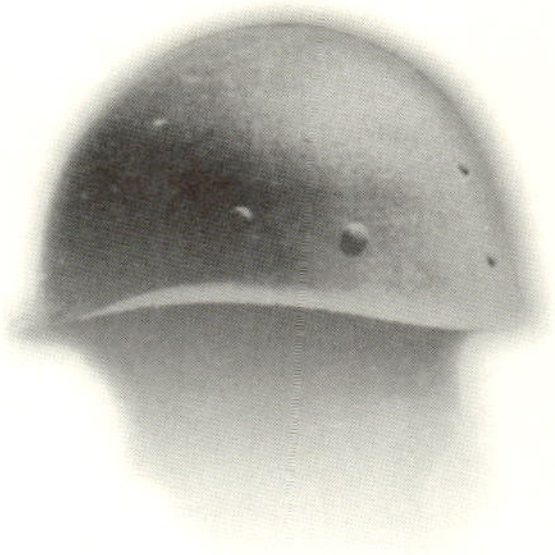

Chapter Twelve

Dad's Footprint

When Dad was on his first sick leave in 1946, among the things he did was visit relatives. He had cousins on my grandfather's side of the family living in International Falls, Minnesota, so that is one of the places he visited. Dad's brother, Jim, was along on that trip and remembers it being the trip where Dad met my mother. Their cousin, Sterling, was married to my mother's sister, Marie, and they set up Dad and Mom on a blind date. No doubt the relationship that began that spring added impetus for Dad to obtain as many sick leave passes that he could so that his visits home could include trips to International Falls. After one of Dad's visits home, my grandmother mentions in a letter that a letter arrived from the Falls for him and she was forwarding it to him.

Living Again

When World War II ended, Dad was like thousands of other veterans; he wanted to get on with his life. To pick up where their lives left off was not possible in many cases because they had seen too much death, endured too much physical hardship, and experienced too much emotional trauma. Priorities were different and the urgency for those priorities was greater. As Dad's foxhole buddy, R.L. Mays relayed in his letter of May, 1946 to Dad (see Chapter 10), *"Don't ask me how I ever got into anything like that for boy I never had an idea I would be doing anything like that* [referring to his current job]. *I like being at home every night and having a place where I can live in one place all* [the] *time."* R.L. wanted to get a job and enjoy the simple pleasures of a roof over his head and being able to stay in one place. I can imagine Dad had similar yearnings.

Margaret and Edgar Houglum, October 23, 1947.

Dad, Peggy, and me on Dad's 29th birthday, 1951.

His hospitalization had delayed him somewhat, but fortunately he was able to meet his bride-to-be during this time period. Dad and Mom were married in International Falls on October 23, 1947.

For most men, the experience in the military did not endow them with a skill for a specific civilian job; Dad was no exception. For awhile, Dad and Mom lived on the farm with my grandparents. In August 1948 Peggy was born. The urgency for a permanent job increased in 1949 when my mother became pregnant with me. A position of rural mail carrier opened in Twin Valley and Dad applied for the position. On June 20th Dad was appointed as the mail carrier for route 1, a 54.9 mile route that included the rural area primarily east and southeast of Twin Valley. His start date was July 5th at an annual salary of $2,970 plus seven cents per mile of equipment maintenance for using his vehicle.

Dad and Mom bought a house lot on Main Avenue in Twin Valley on June 30th for $,1600 from Geneva and Ben Hovde who lived on the adjacent property to the east. The lot already had an enclosed basement, which provided a place for Mom, Dad, Peggy, and me to live until the house was built on top of the basement. After using about $3,900 of their own savings, Dad and Mom obtained a loan from the Farmer's State Bank in Waubun for $4,000 to complete the construction of the house. It was finished in the spring of 1952. They paid the mortgage off in December 1954 without missing a payment.

Dad and Mom's new house, 1952. The steps weren't added yet.

Dad designed the house, which is not surprising considering that prior to entering the Army he had been studying mechanical engineering. He completed much of the interior structure himself. I remember Mom relating a story of when the house was enclosed and the inside completed to some key point. I'm not sure how much of the inside was finished except Mom said the wood floor and brick fireplace were completed in the living room. To savor this point of completion, the young couple had a romantic fire in the fireplace, no doubt with food and/or wine after the kids were asleep below. How much better could it get for a veteran four years after being seriously wounded: a wife, two children, a new house being completed, a steady job, a romantic evening in front of your own fireplace, and living in the country for which you fought to maintain the freedom to enjoy? This was probably the dream of many soldiers while sitting in a cold, wet foxhole thousands of miles from home and wondering if they would make it back home to live that dream. Dad did.

Picture of Dad taken in front of our house with my sister, Pam, in the basket and me on back. As much as possible, Dad was forgetting the war and looking ahead.

Priorities

There is no doubt that World War II, in some way, changed the lives of practically everyone who lived through it. For the many soldiers like my Dad, who survived and returned home, it may have changed the course of their original plans for their lives because what they deemed precious had changed. Maybe the most precious thing was to live in one place with a roof over their heads every night. For Dad, I think it was being a family man, i.e., husband and father.

One summer day when I was a teenager, I was riding in a car with Dad and a golfing friend of his. We were on our way to play golf at Mahnomen, about twenty miles from Twin Valley. We were traveling along County Road 29 near Faith, Minnesota. Dad was in the front seat with his friend who was driving; I was alone in the backseat. I don't remember what they were discussing and don't know if they knew that I was listening, but I heard my Dad's friend ask my Dad if he ever regretted not going back to college to become a mechanical engineer after the war. My Dad said that he had thought about that same question before, but he figured that if he had gone back to college he probably would not have gotten married for a while so that he would be free to focus on college. Dad continued, saying that not being married to Margaret and not having his kids would not have been a better life for him. So, he said, "no," he did not regret the decision of not returning to college.

That portion of the conversation is the only thing I remember about that golf outing, not any other part of their conversation, or my golf score. Dad's response must have been important to me even at that time. The war had changed Dad's priorities and what he now considered precious… and that included me.

Dad and Mom

Dad and Mom lived in their house for over fifty years. They had six children. Dad was a rural mail carrier for thirty-six years, driving over a million miles on his route without an accident. As discussed in Chapter 1, Dad was a very active member of the community and both he and Mom contributed to this small town, U.S.A. in many ways. They lived a full life together with children and grandchildren, Dad living to see great grandchildren. People in the community showed him respect and honor due to his contribution to his family, community, and country.

How Will We Turn Out?

So that is how Dad's life turned out. Was it the battle for freedom that gave him the dedication to see his small community thrive? Was it living for months with the possibility that he may never live to have a wife or family that gave him the desire to be a dedicated family man? Was it the near-death experience that made him change his ambition from being a mechanical engineer to become a rural mail carrier in a small town?

Fifty years later, at their annual 4th of July gathering, the three brothers celebrate the independence for which they served, 1994.

We all will leave some imprint on this life. Dad left his on his country, his family, and his community. As mentioned in Chapter 2, Dad received a souvenir pamphlet from his teacher at Cheerful Nook country school by which to remember the 1931-1932 school year. The title of the pamphlet is "Lest We Forget,," with this poem by Henry W. Longfellow on the front cover:

Lives of great men all remind us
We can make our lives sublime,
And, departing, leave behind us
Footprints on the sands of time.
- Henry W. Longfellow

Dad undoubtedly read the poem when he received this parting gift as he ended 5th grade, but he surely didn't realize at such a young age that it was prophetic for how his life would turn out.

EndNotes

[1] Keefer, Louis E. *The Army Specialized Training Program In World War II.* http://www.pierce-evans.org/ASTP%20in%20WWII.htm . Accessed 7/12/2009.

[2] Volstorff, Vivian V. *The Winds of Change,* an autobiography of South Dakota State University's last Dean of Women. Co-editors, J.L. Petersen, J.O. Pedersen. Pine Hill Press, Inc., Sioux Falls, South Dakota. 2000.

[3] *Combat History of the 324th Infantry Regiment, 44th Infantry Division,* Army & Navy Publishing Co., Baton Rouge, LA. 1946.

[4] 44th Infantry Division. http://efour4ever.com/44thdivision/home.htm.

[5] The Camp Phillips Story. http://www.geocities.com/EnchantedForest/creek/7185/phillips.html. Accessed 9/5/2009

[6] National Postal Museum. www.postalmuseum.si.edu/exhibits/2d2a_vmail.html. Accessed 9/9/2009.

[7] Invasion of Normandy. http://en.wikipedia.org/w/index.php?title=Invasion_of_Normandy&printables=yes. Accessed 9/10/2009.

[8] *Combat History 44th Infantry Division 1944-1945,* Albert Love Enterprises, Atlanta, 1946.

[9] Information provided by John Kregel from his interview of Edgar Houglum, November 3, 2000.

[10] Bonn, Keith E. *When the Odds Were Even,* Ballantine Books, New York, 2006.

[11] Whiting, Charles *The Other Battle of the Bulge, Operation Northwind,* Spellmount, Ltd. Publishers, Great Britain, 2007.

[12] Personal communication, Clifford Van Nest, March 14, 2010.

Appendix

These are the names of people who wrote cards and letters to Dad while he was in the Army. Certainly, other people also wrote to Dad, but those letters evidently have been lost.

Anderson, Andy
Anker, Mr. and Mrs. Elmerk
Berglioth, from Flom (no last name)
Blake, Donavon
Braaten, Melvin and Clara
Chap, Joseph P.
Clara and Kenny (Flom postmark; no last name)
Darlene (an old friend)
Duncan, Helen C.
Ekvall, "Grandpa" (Flom postmark; no first name)
Gene (friend from NDSC; Hunter, ND postmark; no last name)
Harmon, Loren
Harold (military friend in San Francisco; no last name)
Hendrickson, Mr. and Mrs. Eldor
Hilda, and Andrew (Flom postmark; no last name)
Houglum, Alma
Houglum, Jim
Houglum, Joe H.
Houglum, Joseph
Houglum, Monroe
Houglum, Robert
Houglum, Thelma
Jacobsen, Mrs. John
Jacobson, Mr. and Mrs. Nels
Jesness, Bette
Jesness, Hildur

Jesness, Mutt
Jesness, Selvina
Jesness, Shirley
Johnson, Edwin A.
Mays, R.L.
Merlyn (friend from NDSC; no last name)
Meyer, Emil and Mildred
Meyer, Joyce
Meyer, Lois Ann
Morgan, Ruth (Mrs. G.O.)
Ommodt, Arla
Ommodt, Donald
Ommodt, Henry and Mable
Thompson, Thora and Theo
Wangen, Ebba
Wingest, Elizabeth L. (Lucille)

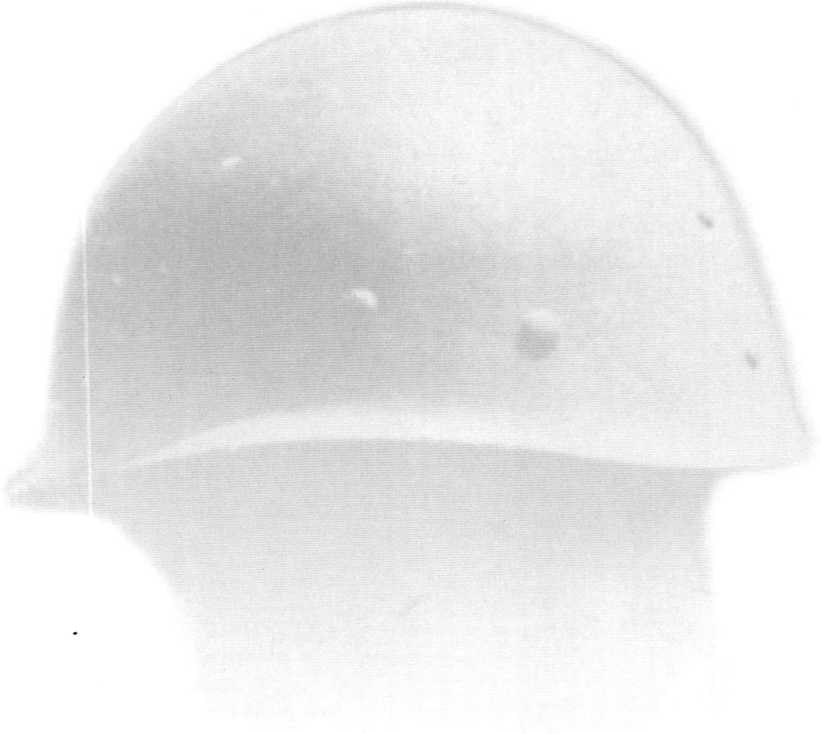